MW01074666

THE WICCAN REDE

Other Books by the Author

THE WICCAN REDE

COUPLETS OF THE
LAW, TEACHINGS, AND
ENCHANTMENTS

MARK VENTIMIGLIA

CITADEL PRESS
Kensington Publishing Corp.
www.kensingtonbooks.com

CITADEL PRESS BOOKS
are published by

Kensington Publishing Corp.
850 Third Avenue
New York, NY 10022

Scott Cunningham, *Wicca: A Guide for the Solitary Practitioner* (Llewellyn,
St. Paul, MN, 1988). Excerpts used by permission.

Edred Thorsson: *Futhark: A Handbook of Rune Magic* (Samuel Weiser, York
Beach, ME, 1984). Excerpts used by permission.

Edred Thorsson: *Runelore: A Handbook of Esoteric Runology* (Samuel Weiser,
York Beach, ME, 1987). Excerpts used by permission.

All Kensington titles, imprints, and distributed lines are available at special
quantity discounts for bulk purchases for sales promotions, premiums, fund-
raising, educational, or institutional use. Special book excerpts or customized
printings can also be created to fit specific needs. For details, write or phone
the office of the Kensington special sales manager: Kensington Publishing
Corp., 850 Third Avenue, New York, NY 10022, attn: Special Sales Depart-
ment, phone 1-800-221-2647.

CITADEL PRESS and the Citadel logo are Reg. U.S. Pat. & TM Off.

First printing: June 2003

10 9 8 7 6 5 4 3 2

Printed in the United States of America

Library of Congress Control Number: 2002115412

ISBN 0-8065-2517-7

MY TEACHER and friend, Raymond Buckland, once said that the Ultimate Deity is some genderless force that is so far beyond our comprehension that we can have only the vaguest understanding of its being. Yet we know it's there. Some call this force God; others call it Goddess. There are many names associated with this force: Odin, Freya, Cernunnos, Aphrodite, Enki, Amen-Ra, and Isis, just to list a few. It is to this supreme life force, the Ultimate Truth, that this book is dedicated.

જ

Contents

س

PREFACE

THE REASON WHY I wrote *The Wiccan Rede* is simple: There has never been a book written or published solely concentrating on its deep and meaningful teachings, and so I felt that there was a definite need. On any visit to your local library or bookstore's New Age and occult section, you will find volumes upon volumes of Wiccan spellbooks, formularies, grimoires, and recipe books, but not one book has ever been published discussing our one main *Law*. To me, this is extremely sad.

Many New Age and Wiccan books casually mention the Rede in passing, usually haphazardly, and most witches can even quote this epic poem, yet how many of us actually live the philosophy it teaches? In our conversations, we hear common phrases like, "*in perfect love, in perfect trust,*" and "*mind the Threefold Law,*" but what do these sayings actually mean, and how are we, as Wiccans, supposed to incorporate them into our daily lives? Even the main tenet of our gentle faith, "*an ye harm none, do as thou will,*" has been so grossly misinterpreted by the masses that many so-called witches feel that they can do just about anything they want without suffering any adverse consequences. To prove this point, we see many New Age books teaching manipulative spells for gaining love, wealth, and happiness, which, coincidentally, goes against everything morally and ethically right. Sure, magick is our birthright, and we have the Goddess-given right to practice magick to obtain happiness, but before we work our magick spells and incantations, we must weigh all of the consequences to be sure that our workings *harm none*.

However, the Wiccan Rede is much more than just a collection of rules to follow. It is not a set of commandments, but a complete learning system. Take, for instance, the phrase "*nine woods in the cauldron go*." Here the Rede is instructing in the age-old teaching of herbal lore. And in another area of the poem, we study the intimate details of magick itself when we learn to "*cast the circle thrice about, to keep unwelcomed spirits out*." Every sentence of the Rede contains deep and meaningful philosophical wisdom, and it is our duty as witches to extract that wisdom and then put it into daily practice.

Many pagans seem to focus on Wicca's occult and magickal properties and almost totally forget that Wicca is primarily a religion. The Wiccan Rede fills a much-needed void in today's witchcraft community, and I feel that every practicing Wiccan, whether solitary or coven member, should have a copy of *The Wiccan Rede* in their personal library. It will greatly enhance your understanding of the basic philosophy of Wicca and add much to your spiritual life as well.

Roxana, Illinois

ACKNOWLEDGMENTS

I WOULD LIKE to take this time to thank the following people for helping me whilst working on the manuscript for this handbook. Without their continued support, this book would never have materialized: Jenny Westcott, Scott Davis, Scott Ventimiglia, Kurt Ventimiglia, Dallas Bennett, Raymond Buckland, Andrea Voke, and my wonderful parents, Walter and Sandra Ventimiglia.

I would also like to send a great deal of thanks to my editors Bruce Bender, Miles Lott, and Margaret Wolf, as well as everyone at Kensington Publishing Corporation who took the time and patience to work with me on this very demanding project.

THE WICCAN REDE

INTRODUCTION

Humanity's Original Religion

CONTRARY TO WHAT biblical scholars profess,[1] the human race has existed on the planet Earth for at least four million years.[2] Through archaeological research and findings, scientists have amassed documented proof that for the majority of our existence, humanity has practiced religion. Paleolithic-age cave drawings[3] of primitive humans executing both religious as well as magickal rites have been found by archeologists, proving conclusively that the human race has been interested in supernatural as well as spiritual phenomena from our

---

[1] Many Judeo-Christian theologians claim that their Bible is the one true and literal recorded history of the human race, and that it defines human existence on our planet as being only six thousand years old.

[2] The Lucy (australopithecine afarensis) fossils, which were recently discovered by D. C. Johanson on the surface of Pliocene deposits in Ethiopia, date to four million years old.

[3] Forbidden Archeology, Michael Cremo, Bhaktivedanta Book Trust, 1993; Dictionary of Art and Archaeology, J. W. Mollett, Bracken Books, 1994; The Amateur Archaeologist's Handbook, Maurice Robbins, Harper and Row, 1981.

earliest origins.[4] Many of these scientific discoveries have given us the ability to successfully trace, through an unbroken line of tradition from prehistoric times to our present age, the evolution of human religious beliefs.

All primitive and aboriginal religious practices and beliefs are shamanistic in origin.[5] The main ideology structuring all shamanistic paganism is the inherent belief in a sky deity, depicted as *father*, and an earth deity, seen as *mother*. These two ideas evolve slowly, developing additional and secondary traits over the centuries, ultimately becoming independent entities or Gods. In time, a complete pantheon is created that originated from these two primal forces of nature. Each God is then ascribed specific attributes pertaining to certain natural phenomena. Knowing this, we can see

---

[4]In September of 1991, the mummified Otze man was discovered by two German hikers half buried in the snow near the Similaun Glacier at an altitude of 13,000 feet. The remains contained an axe, flint knife, long bow, and arrows, as well as a birch bark container and stone jewelry that may have been used as an amulet or talisman. While the mummy dates to only 5000 years old, other discoveries in the area indicate that humans have inhabited the area for more than 50,000 years.

[5]Shamanism and Animism are nature-respecting religious philosophies where a spirit, or a god, is attributed to each of the natural forces of nature. Simply put, one god controls the wind, another god controls the rain, a different god controls the growth of vegetation, and so on. Witchcraft is a shamanistic religion.

that originally, these two primal forces were nothing more than natural energies occurring randomly throughout the cosmos, but in time, they progressively developed independent traits and personalities as human society became more sophisticated.

This is not to say that humanity *created* the Gods, for in fact we did not. The God-force was present in the universe long before the advent of humanity. It is from this God-force that all matter, and hence all life, was spawned. Based on our observation of natural phenomena, the human race simply created an idea of a god and then attached that idea to the aforementioned natural phenomena. However, in doing so, a thought-form[6] is born and an individual God comes into being, fully independent and conscious. Simply put, we were created by the God-force, yet we organized that same God-force into a system that we could readily comprehend.

Humanity's Need for Gods and Religion

Humanity's need for its Gods and religion is a very personal and intimate one. From the perspective of the

---

[6] A thought-form is a psychic phenomenon that is created by the mental and emotional beliefs of an individual or society. Where this belief is concentrated, through the adherence of religious and magickal rites by practitioners, the thought-form grows in strength and intelligence until it becomes an independent and conscious entity.

primitive mind, the material world was a very terrifying place to live; thunderstorms roared throughout the dark night and forest fires often raged for days, weeks, or even months, consuming everything in their path. Other natural disasters such as droughts and famines also had to be endured. Through observation of these natural forces, primitive tribes tried to offset these catastrophes by communicating with these forces directly, either through magickal or religious rituals.

The human intellect is not capable of comprehending the God-force directly. This is true even today with all of our vast technological breakthroughs. This is also why primitive tribes *invented* deities that represented the terrific forces of nature that they had to deal with on a daily basis.

Scientific observations of behavioral traits of the human race, through controlled anthropological and archeological research, have revealed much concerning the differences between how individuals, as well as groups, think, believe, and act. Every person, whether individual or part of a group, discovers a deity with whom they can identify; a God or Goddess that can be petitioned in times of need. Religion, and a belief in a God and Goddess on which one's hopes and desires can be attached, give spiritual comfort in an otherwise terrifying world.

The Basics of Duality

From the very beginning of our religious observations, the human race has understood the necessity of religious *duality*. Since shamanistic paganism[7] is a nature-revering religious practice based on observation, it is easy to ascertain the reasons behind this belief in duality. Everywhere in nature, one observes the energetic polarities of both male and female. The attributes of the male-female energy, as the all-pervasive life-giving force, are witnessed through such simple acts as watching a seed drop from a tree and taking root or the miraculous birth of an animal. It was only natural that the primitive mind saw a connection between these two energies and the overall forces of nature, and included them in their religious system. This perfect balance in religious spirituality guaranteed health and happiness in everyday life.

However, where there is an imbalance in nature, disease and decay take root. Recently, for just the past few thousand years, we have witnessed a gross imbalance in religion, and a decay in our society unlike anything we have ever experienced has been the result. Most likely, this is due to humanity's ignorance of sophisticated natural laws, and can also be seen in the recent adherence

[7]Witchcraft.

to monotheism, which, incidentally, completely ignores the necessary male-female balance.

Oppression and Religious Prejudice

As there is a balance in nature, there needs to be a balance in religious philosophy as well. This observation cannot be overstated. With the God, there must be the polarity opposite of the Goddess, or a grave imbalance will originate, creating an unnatural vacuum, where a void will develop and ultimate chaos will result. We can see the proof of this even today, where the idea of a one true and universal male God has created countless suffering throughout the world for the past few millenniums.

Humanity has reached a very critical point in its evolution. When the mystery and wonder of our natural world began to fade at the dawning of our Industrial Revolution, and with the advent of the atomic age, we became arrogant. With that arrogance came greed, the desire to dominate and control others, and a lust for ultimate supremacy in the universe. In essence, we didn't need the Gods anymore. But rather than discard them, we reorganized them into our own machines of oppression and control. Through this invention, religious prejudice was born, under the guise of monotheism.

The Gods of the Old Religion Become
the Devils of the New Religion

In absolute monotheism, there is no personal freedom of worship. The practitioner of these cults has only one grim choice, to bow down to a male authoritarian figure who imposes upon his followers a list of unbreakable laws, keeping them in complete submission with threats based on such philosophically unrealistic ideas as absolute good and absolute evil.[8]

The concept of one God being all good and a different God being all evil was, and is, unheard of in shamanistic paganism and witchcraft. Our Gods are similar to ourselves in many ways, for their personalities are as complex as their powers are great. The simplistic concept of a God being only one certain way was beyond the comprehension of the primitive mind, and this should not come as a surprise, for simple observation can show us the extreme diversity in nature. One day we experience a gentle rain that nourishes, and another day we witness a violent storm that destroys. Even people have their good moods as well as their bad

---

[8]The idea of a one *all good* god and one *all evil* god was adopted by Zoroaster, a Persian religious leader living in the seventh century B.C.E. This doctrine was later adopted by both Christianity and Mithraism.

moods, so why not the Gods? It makes perfect sense that the Gods are capable of both good deeds as well as mischievous deeds. They are living entities, and like all things in the universe, they are subject to the same natural laws as we are. Just like us, they grow, learn, and evolve. The only difference is that the Gods are higher on the evolutionary ladder, and so we have a tendency to put them on a high pedestal.

It is often said that the Gods of the old religion become the devils of the new religion. We can clearly see an example of this in the Christian invention of Satan. Nowhere in the biblical texts of the Old Testament is there a description of this entity, other than that of the snake in the Garden of Eden, yet modern-day priests and preachers of this cult have drawn us a perfect picture of a mythical beast with goat's hooves and horns.

Early in the Christian Church's struggle for supremacy, there developed a practice of weeding out, at any cost, the competition to the new religion. Since pagan deities like Pan and Cernunnos were horned, and since paganism was in direct competition with the new and struggling church, these old Gods became the target of their attacks. The church created an all-evil deity in the image of the old Gods with the hope of turning people from paganism to Christianity.

The Fallacies of the
Middle-Eastern Texts

Contrary to popular belief, monotheism was not the original religious idea of the human race, nor was it the invention of Judeo-Christianity. Monotheism was created by the Egyptian pharaoh Amenhotep III of the XVIII Dynasty.

A corrupt and greedy hierarchy of Egyptian priests came into power during Amenhotep's reign, and in direct response to this corruption, he instituted a religion with only one god, *Aton*.[9] This new religion, established through the workings of a violent and bloody revolution, was completely devoid of any female deities. From this creation, seventy-seven years later, Judaism was born, through Moses's development of the Jehovah cult,[10] which basically stems from the Egyptian Aton

---

[9] Aton, an imposing male deity, was a direct by-product of the Egyptian male-dominated society and culture.

[10] Amenhotep's reign was from 1412 B.C. to 1376 B.C. His son and successor, Amenhotep IV, also called Ikhnaton or Akhenaten, ruled from 1376 B.C. to 1359 B.C., and continued his father's monotheistic religion. Tutankhamen, who was considered an incarnation of the Living God, and whose name literally means "Living image of Amen the Hidden God," reigned from 1359 B.C. to 1350 B.C., succeeded Amenhotep IV, and restored polytheism to Egypt. Moses was alleged to have been living during the reign of Ramses II, from 1304 B.C. to 1237 B.C., over a century later.

cult. Christianity and Islam, both heretical offshoots of Judaism, also adopted this male-dominated monotheism as a result of their male-dominated culture.

The problem in today's world is the adherence to these foreign doctrines and dogmas. As was documented earlier, D. C. Johanson's discovery of the *Lucy* fossils, which are the oldest human fossils on record, were found in Pliocene deposits in Ethiopia, Africa, and *not* in the Middle East between the Tigris and Euphrates Rivers as the Judeo-Christian Bible would lead one to believe.

Many people also turn to the various ancient Sumerian[11] and Babylonian texts for proof of monotheism's superiority, but again, an accurate and unbiased translation of these documents simply does not exist. It is common knowledge that many, if not all of these texts, were translated by Judeo-Christian scholars and much of this literature has been adapted to suit their particular needs.

One interesting piece of information, proving the misconceptions of the various ancient texts, comes to us from the *Papyrus of Nu*.[12] Contained in this ancient

---

[11] In an old Sumerian tale, we see the deity Tiamat, personified as female, as being evil and eventually destroyed by the war-like male deity, Marduk.

[12] The *Papyrus of Nu* is dated to the XVIII Dynasty and is currently housed in the British Museum. It is listed as manuscript #10,477.

Egyptian papyrus are forty-two entries, arranged systematically as a sort of prayer, which correspond directly to certain Egyptian laws. Ironically enough, the papyrus reads identically, in some places, to that of Moses's *Ten Commandments*, yet predates the Mosaic era by some seventy-seven years! Does this mean that Moses did not receive Jehovah's Law when he ascended the mountain of Sinai? Does this mean that he pilfered those commandments from Egyptian religious archives? This is just one of many accounts that prove the ancient texts have been falsified, hidden, or completely deleted from public record.

Oppressive Religious Programming

Many modern Wiccans suffer from religious programming. Christianity has spread to most parts of the world, and has sent its roots and tendrils deep in the psychic and emotional fabric of our society. The average person seeking spiritual freedom through shamanistic paganism and witchcraft must continuously battle the subconscious programming put into employment by the Christian Church centuries ago. Like any thought-form, if enough people believe in it, it will grow and gain strength. Whether the thought-form is good or evil makes no difference; it is still a very real entity.

Understanding the Wiccan Rede on a personal and intimate level will help one overcome this negative programming, see through the religious prejudices, and gain the overall strength one needs to live a truly spiritual life.

Wicca and the Modern Witchcraft Movement

So today, with the advent of the new millennium, we have come full circle. We are witches; we have returned to Earth. The Earth is our mother and we cherish her, and her eternal consort is our divine father, the spirit of life itself. This complete duality is worshipable, not one over the other, but the two in complete balance and unison. No longer do we seek to be oppressed by a religious doctrine and dogma that violates every known natural law. No longer will we stand for religious arrogance and ignorance heaped upon us by a chauvinistic society and culture. No longer will we embrace a deity that directly opposes everything good and wholesome and pure.

So, what is it to be a practitioner of the Wiccan faith in the new century? Being a Wiccan goes further than mere religious beliefs and practices. Today's witches are ever mindful of issues like religious freedom and human rights, animal rights, environmental policies of governments, deforestation problems, and ocean and air pollution problems, just to name a few. While many of us are activists, we are not martyrs. We should teach what we have learned, and that teaching is best done through example. For too many centuries, religious ideas have been spread through the use of threats and violence; Wicca is a gentle faith and must not be proselytized in this manner. Even though the Wiccan Rede[13] is twenty-six couplets long, the entire philosophy of our Way is summed up in its final line: "*An it harm none, do as thou will.*"

My only piece of advice is this: Learn as much as you can about Wicca, witchcraft, and your chosen tradition. Study practical magick techniques, as well as religious ritual formulas. Practice a lifestyle that peacefully co-exists within the laws of nature, and any time a doubt crosses your mind, ask yourself one simple question: *Will my actions cause harm to another living being?*

---

[13] The actual historical authenticity of the Wiccan Rede has been in dispute for some time. It is believed that a member of the Gardnerian tradition penned the epic poem a few decades ago, but this cannot be confirmed. Even though the Wiccan Rede does not come to us from antiquity, that fact does not take away from its timeless wisdom and intimate teachings. Herein lies the fundamental foundation for true spiritual growth.

THE WICCAN REDE

Bide the *Wiccan Law* ye must; in perfect love,
in perfect trust.

Ye must live an' let live, fairly take an' fairly give.

Cast the *circle* thrice about, to keep unwelcomed
spirits out.

To bind the spell well every time, let the spell
be spoken in rhyme.

Soft of eye an' light of touch, speak ye little
an' listen much.

Deosil go by waxing moon, chanting out the
Seax-Wiccan Runes.

Widdershins go by waning moon, chanting out thy
baneful tune.

When the *Lady's moon* is new, kiss the hand
to her times two.

When the moon rides at her peak, then thou
heart's desire seek.

Heed the north wind's mighty gale, lock the door
an' trim the sail.

When the wind comes from the south, love will kiss
thee on the mouth.

When the wind blows from the west,
departed spirits have no rest.

When the wind blows from the east, expect the new
an' set the feast.

Nine woods in the cauldron go, burn them fast
an' burn them slow.

Elder be the *Lady's tree*, burn it not or cursed
thou'll be.

When the *wheel* begins to turn, let the *Beltane*
fires burn.

When the *wheel* has turned to *Yule*, light the log
an' the *Horned One* rules.

Heed ye flower, bush an' tree, by the *Lady*, bless'd be.

Where the rippling waters go, cast a stone
an' truth thou'll know.

When ye have an' hold a need, hearken not
to others' greed.

With a fool no season spend, lest ye be counted
as her friend.

Merry meet an' merry part, bright the cheeks
an' warm the heart.

Mind the *Threefold Law* ye should, three times bad
an' three times good.

When misfortune is enow, wear the witches' star
on thy brow.

True in love forever be, lest thy lover's false to thee.

Eight words the *Wiccan Rede* fulfill:
An ye harm none, do as thou will.

〜

1

IN PERFECT LOVE

THE FIRST COUPLET of the Wiccan Rede teaches: "*Bide the Wiccan Law ye must; in perfect love, in perfect trust.*" There is a very good reason why the poem begins as such, and if we look to the history surrounding witchcraft, the meaning of this first and very important lesson becomes quite clear.

In its early years, the Christian religion was slow growing. The old pagan religions were seen by the new Church as their main rival and the ultimate threat to its overall existence. So, out of the necessity of survival, the founding fathers of the new Christian religion organized their first wave of assault on paganism with the hope of converting the entire populace to its new religious doctrine. However, there was not the immediate mass conversion to Christianity that history often suggests. The new religion was just that, a newly created, man-made religion. It did not evolve slowly over many millenniums, as did paganism. In fact, often entire nations were classified as Christian countries when in truth it was only their leaders who had adopted the new faith. Throughout the whole of Europe, and Britain as well, paganism continued to exist, more or less, during the first thousand years of Christianity.

From as early as the fourth century, pagans everywhere were under heavy pressure from the Catholic Church to abandon their ancestral faith and convert to Christianity. At first the Church sent its bishops, as ambassadors of Rome, to the courts of the pagan kings of Europe and Britain to request their allegiance to the Catholic faith. If the king would not give in to the pressures set upon him, then the Church would often petition the queen, who would usually relent and convert to the new religion. It was then the queen's duty to convert her husband. Sometimes this worked and sometimes it did not. Often, after a king would convert to Christianity and then later be slain in battle, his heir would abandon the new religion and return to the old pagan faith of his ancestors. This led to an all-out assault on paganism by the Catholic Church, thus beginning the dark and bloody times of the persecutions.

Pope Gregory the Great attempted a mass conversion of Europe by ordering all pagan temples to be razed, and then he sanctioned the building of Catholic churches on their foundations. Catholic bishops were instructed to smash all pagan statues, and after the new churches were built, sprinkle holy water throughout the structure, rededicating it to the new religion and its one true God.

In 1484, Pope Innocent VIII wrote a Papal Bull condemning witchcraft as heresy and commanding the sentence of death on all convicted witches. Two years later, the German monks Heinrich Kramer and Jakob Sprenger published their infamous *Malleus Maleficarum*, which graphically outlined many heinous torture techniques to be used on individuals suspected of witchcraft. These two actions were not isolated events. The Christian Church continued its bloody persecution of paganism and its roots penetrated deep into the fabric of European culture. After some time, it seemed that they had finally succeeded in stamping out all traces of paganism in Europe and Britain.

Incidentally, up until these terrible days, paganism was purely an open and oral tradition. Even if their kings did succumb to Christianity, more often than not, the common population continued to remain faithful to the pagan roots of their ancestors. During this time, it was a common practice among coven witches to take an *Oath of Secrecy*. This oath was a sincere pledge of extreme *loyalty*, to each other as well as to one's faith. Such emphasis was placed on this loyalty that the *Oath of Secrecy* came to guarantee a high degree of security during these terrible times. Should one witch be caught, even under severe torture, he or she would not divulge the whereabouts of another witch or coven.

Thankfully, witches living and practicing the Old Religion in the twenty-first century do not have to worry about being convicted of heresy and tortured or burned at the stake. However, loyalty to one's coven and fidelity to one's religion should be of paramount importance. To abide by the Wiccan law, and consequently its principles and philosophies, we must forever remain loyal to the main teachings of the religion, which are summed up in the final couplet of the poem, "*An it harm none.*"

If we truly abide by this one supreme and universal law, we learn the ultimate meaning of the phrase, "*in perfect love, in perfect trust.*" Love and trust coexist eternally within the boundaries of loyalty. To love unconditionally is to remain forever faithful in that love, and where there is unconditional love, there is also unconditional trust. We must never do anything that will violate that trust.

When one takes up the practice of Wicca, whether being formally initiated into a coven or informally initiating oneself as a solitary practitioner, we must be ever mindful of the family we are joining. The coven members are your brothers and sisters and the Goddess and the God are your eternal parents; there is an eternal bond of love and trust that originates from such a relationship. It should be understood that we must always act in love toward all of creation.

Required Reading for This Chapter

Buckland, Raymond. *The Tree: Complete Book of Saxon Witchcraft*. Samuel Weiser, 1974.

Cunningham, Scott. *Wicca: A Guide for the Solitary Practitioner*. Llewellyn, 1988.

Gardner, Gerald B. *Witchcraft Today*. Rider, 1954.

2

GIVE AND TAKE

THE SECOND COUPLET of the Wiccan Rede teaches: "*Ye must live an' let live, fairly take an' fairly give.*" In its utmost simplicity, this lesson stresses the value and sanctity of all life, and the important necessities of abstinence from theft and for generosity and compassion.

In human society, we claim to have made life and the preservation of that life our top priority. Our laws reflect this mentality, but they do so in a very hypocritical manner. Humanity recognizes the value and sanctity of human life, but it stops there. Plants, animals, and even the earth herself are expendable in the minds of most human beings, in relation to the value and sanctity of human life. This is a gross philosophical imbalance, and one that has caused many problems and suffering throughout the ages.

In many of the world's sacred and so-called revealed scriptures, we find that humanity was given the gift of life by the very Gods, and because of this belief, humanity has grown arrogant. We have begun to feel supreme on the Earth, as if human life were in some way divine and sacred, and more holy than any other form of life. This is simply not true. While, in truth, the Gods did grant us the gift of life, it was also these same Gods that fashioned the material world and gave life to the plants and the animals as well. Through observation one will discover a simple formula: *Since the Gods created humanity, then human life is sacred and divine, but so too is all life, since the Gods created all that exists!* We must keep this in mind while contemplating the second couplet of the Wiccan Rede.

Many human rights activists advocate a liberal ideal called *absolute freedom,* yet the very concept of absolute freedom is a myth. It simply does not exist. There is no such thing as absolute freedom, since if one practices freedom absolutely, a vacuum is created and somewhere in the world, another's freedom is hindered. This has been one of the major problems with the human way of thinking. We all want to increase the standard of our lives, but we must not do so at the cost of others. In today's world, this is precisely what is happening. In many Third World countries, an entire nation is kept in poverty while working as slaves to provide luxuries for the world's wealthy nations.

A better philosophy would be to practice *restrained freedom.* Yes, it seems like a contradiction in terms, but if one were to closely examine the concept behind it, one would find out that it is truly a compassionate idea. Each individual must evaluate the amount of freedom that is necessary for an acceptable standard of living. We must not be gluttons and overuse our abilities, wasting what we have, and caring not for others. We must restrain our freedom to the point where we can still enjoy our life, but not at the cost of others. Take, for instance, the idea of a fast food sandwich. How much does that cost? I am not speaking of a monetary value here, but of a moral and ethical standard. So, you enjoy your hamburgers? Have you ever stopped to think about how much pain and suffering goes into the production of that sandwich? For every hamburger you consume, a living creature had to die, and usually very horribly. These creatures are much like you and me; they are capable of feeling happiness, fear, love, anger, and pain. Yet, we exterminate them by the millions for the satisfaction of our greedy little stomachs. It is very sad, indeed.

As the Wiccan Rede states ever so clearly, "*Ye must live an' let live.*" We should grant the same standard of life to all life, and cease from the hideous theft of resources from throughout our dark past for the raising of our own standard of living.

The second part of this teaching is eternalized in the phrase *"fairly take an' fairly give."* When one steals from the Universe, it is as if one is stealing from one's own mother. These words ring true throughout the ages and one should contemplate their deep and eternal meaning. Look at this example for a moment: Originally, there were eight million square miles of tropical rain forest encircling the Earth. Due to humanity's greed, more than half has been burned, bulldozed, and destroyed. Currently, only about three and a half million square miles remain. When one stops to realize that the tropical rain forests of the Earth provide between twenty-five to forty percent of all pharmaceutical products,[1] we then begin to understand what a grand scale our ignorance has reached. This, of course, does not even scratch the surface of the gross injustice that we do to the other inhabitants of the rain forests, such as animals and aboriginal humans.

As Wiccans, we should contemplate daily on how we can increase the mindfulness of our compassion and generosity, so that not only *our* life is enriched, but all other life as well. The following short prayer is a good

[1] Currently, three thousand plants have been discovered to contain anti-cancer properties, and of these, seventy percent inhabit the tropical rain forests of our planet.

way to thank the Goddess and the God, our eternal mother and father, for our life, as well as instilling in our heart the interconnectedness of all life.

A Prayer of Thanksgiving[2]

Dear Mother, my eternal Goddess, you are inherent in the Green Earth. I know and understand that we are each a manifestation of the living being of you, the Earth, our Mother. Thank you for giving me this physical body, this gift of yourself, which you have given freely. Thank you for being my foundation, the substance of all that is.

Dear Father, my eternal God, you are the life of the Earth's substance. I know and understand that we are all linked with all of creation as parts of one living organism. Thank you for giving me this most sacred gift, the gift of life. Blessed be.

The Natural Diet

In keeping with the thought that all life is sacred and divine, I would like to touch on the benefits of a natu-

---

[2]The original title of this prayer is *Morning Prayer of Thanksgiving*, and is found on page 49 of *The Wiccan Prayer Book*. Ventimiglia, Mark. *The Wiccan Prayer Book*. New York, Citadel Press, 2000.

ral diet that exemplifies the principles of the Wiccan Rede and its deep philosophical teachings.

Since the physical body is the primary vehicle while existing in the material world, it makes perfect sense to safeguard that vehicle accordingly. In today's fast-paced world, many of us do not take the time to consider the consequences of a poor and inadequate diet. In the worst case scenario, especially in America where the majority of the population is grossly overweight, most people live to eat, rather than eating to live.

In this short section, we will look at the various dietary health requirements of the human body, physical as well as spiritual, and examine the consequences of neglecting these requirements.

Physical

Like all machines, the physical human body needs energy in order to function properly. We obtain this energy through the air we breathe, the water we drink, and the food we eat. While we can do very little to guarantee the purity of the air we breathe, we are not that helpless when it comes to securing quality food and water. One can easily purchase bottled water and organically grown fruits, vegetables, whole grains, and cereals at many health food chains.

The body needs food to supply the energy needed for healthy cell growth and tissue repair. Understand that regardless of the quality of one's diet, these two requirements will be met, even at the ultimate cost of overall health. If energy in the form of food were eliminated, the body would simply devour itself.

There are four essential components of the kind of well-balanced, natural diet needed for optimal health. They are proteins, carbohydrates, fats, and minerals. It should be remembered that these four elements are found in larger proportions in vegetable matter than in animal tissue. For example, nuts, peas, beans, milk, and cheese contain a large percentage of nitrogenous matter, whereas wheat, oats, rice, and potatoes contain mainly carbohydrates.

Nearly all the protein foods and vegetable oils furnish important fats, while the valuable organic mineral elements of iron, potassium, etc., are mostly found in vegetable matter. Fruits and vegetables supply much of these vital organic minerals and also help in keeping an alkaline reserve in the bloodstream. This is crucial in sustaining the blood's capacity for transporting carbon dioxide to the lungs for elimination.

Aside from containing important minerals, vegetables are also the most important source for vitamins. Vegetables that can be eaten raw, such as lettuce, spinach, cabbage, and tomatoes, contain the three main vitamins required by the human body: Vitamins A, B, and C. During cooking, keep in mind that vitamins A and B are not affected by boiling, but frying will destroy them. Vitamin C, which is indispensable for healthy bones and teeth, is found only in fruits and green leafy vegetables.

Where protein is concerned, milk is a complete food. Therefore, a diet containing milk and dairy products, fresh fruits, leafy vegetables, and whole grains is the ideal diet for all of humanity. This simply means that human beings are not carnivores nor omnivores, but rather, we are true herbivores by our very physical nature. With a combination of nuts, cereals, plenty of fruits, and vegetables, one obtains all the important vitamins, minerals, proteins, carbohydrates, and fats needed for optimal health.

The intelligent Wiccan not only adheres to a natural diet, but also practices proper mastication and eating habits. Slow and thorough chewing of one's food and an appropriate eating schedule (ie: No eating between meals, etc.) are prerequisites to good dietary health. Once one practices proper mastication, the abnormal appetite that compels one to overeat will steadily decline and one will return to a normal eating schedule. Occasional fasting is also a good idea, especially

during times of illness. Fasting gives the stomach a
chance to rest and the energy once used for digestion
can then be used for recuperation to eliminate the poisons and toxins from the body.

It is common medical knowledge that fresh fruits
and raw vegetables contain the much-needed antiscor-
butic elements that assist in the prevention of disease.
Meat, on the other hand, is related to the contraction of
many diseases such as trichinosis, heart disease, intestinal worms, colon cancer, gout, rheumatism, uric acid
disease, headaches, epilepsy, convulsions, and nervousness, just to name a few. Humans practicing a vegetarian diet, as advised by true Wiccan philosophy, also heal
more quickly than people who consume mainly meat
in their diets. In addition, one reduces the risk of fevers
by diligently following a vegetarian diet.

A major health problem brought on by a meat diet is
uric acid disease. Uric acid deposits in the muscle fibers
of meat cause a considerably large number of ailments
experienced by humans. When uric acid is introduced
into the system, the human body must eliminate its own
manufactured supply, plus the extra supply taken in the
form of meat. This puts a considerable amount of
unnecessary stress on one's system. The amount of uric
acid the human body is capable of eliminating, via the
kidneys, is only about six grains per day. Sixteen ounces

of beef contains approximately fourteen grains of uric acid; liver contains around nineteen grains. As a person's liver and kidneys are not able to deal with the added intake of uric acid, the uneliminated uric acid builds up in the system and becomes a seedbed for disease.

For many years, cholesterol has been linked to various diseases. It is common knowledge that the human body is unable to deal with excessive amounts of animal fat and cholesterol, yet the average American and European diet is heavily laden with both. In a meat-centered diet, where a person eats more cholesterol than is required, the excess can cause serious health problems. It accumulates on the inner walls of arteries and constricts the flow of blood to the heart, which can lead to high blood pressure, heart disease, strokes, and eventually death. On the other hand, medical studies recently undertaken at the University of Milan have shown evidence that vegetable protein actually aids the body in keeping cholesterol levels low.

The major meat-producing companies of the world have flooded the marketplace with literally tons of misinformation. The idea that a high-protein diet is beneficial for good health is pure propaganda. In reality, the opposite is actually true. A diet consisting largely of pure protein in the form of meat, fish, poultry, and eggs contains extremely high levels of cholesterol. The average meat-eating human consumes around 500–600 mg of cholesterol every day, whereas the human body can safely eliminate only up to 100 mg a day. The uneliminated cholesterol then builds up to dangerously high levels in the body.

Many people ask the question "Why are people who eat meat more prone to disease?" This question is a relatively easy one to answer. A simple observation of the human body is all that is needed to fully understand that we are not designed to consume flesh. Some closed-minded persons will argue that humans have canine teeth suitable for tearing flesh, but upon close observation, one will see that this is simply not true. A carnivorous animal's canine teeth are three to four times larger than the other teeth; such is not the case in humans. We also do not possess the musculature, speed, or strength of a carnivorous creature. However, the main reason we are so susceptible to diseases when we consume meat lies in our digestive system. The human intestinal tract is simply not suited for digesting meat. Carnivorous animals have short intestinal tracts that pass the rapidly decaying, toxin-producing meat out of the body quickly. Since vegetable material decays more slowly than meat, herbivores have a longer intestinal tract. The human body has the long intestinal tract of a herbivore, so if one eats meat, the toxins contained in the meat fibers overload the kidneys, which leads to gout, arthritis, rheumatism, heart disease, and cancer.

It is interesting to know that even the professional processing of meat contributes to its disease-enhancing factors. When alive, animal tissue is supple and tender, but soon after death, the flesh begins to harden from the coagulation of the muscle fibers. This causes the meat to become tough, and it does not become tender again until it putrefies. This is why meat is often kept for some time to *ripen*, "cure," or in other words, decay. As already stated, putrefied meat contains many poisonous substances and is the main cause of hypertension and other serious health problems.

After realizing one's true place in nature, we can clearly see that a natural, vegetarian diet helps build resistance to disease and safely prolongs life. Incidentally, all food is originally a by-product of the plant world. The energy found in meat is the balance of what has not been used by the animal. When one eats the flesh of an animal, one is taking vegetable food from the unused portion of the flesh, since vegetable energy is the original source of all meat energy.

Humanity utilizes only the flesh of animals that subsist entirely on plants, namely cows, pigs, sheep, poultry, etc. This fact also mirrors itself in the wild animals that humanity hunts for meat. Humanity does not eat the flesh of meat-eating animals such as lions, tigers, cougars, wolves, etc.; this is further proof that the human body draws recycled energy from the flesh of animals that live on vegetables. Knowing all this, it should be understood that vegetable food, rather than animal food, is the natural diet of a human being.

One last note concerning a meat diet—it is highly unbalanced nutritionally. Diets that contain excess amounts of animal protein are completely lacking in the essential vitamins and minerals needed for optimal function. To offset this fact, many meat eaters opt for the occasional daily vitamin and mineral supplements often seen at health food stores and supermarkets. However, contrary to this practice, it is more beneficial to obtain one's essential nutrients through food rather than from a pill or tablet. It should be understood that over-the-counter drugs and painkillers should be avoided as well.

Drugs numb the body and make the mind sluggish. Pain is the body's way of communicating that there is something wrong in the system. Painkillers simply turn off this important mechanism, thus allowing illnesses to take a stronger hold and gain a foundation, as well as adding to the problem by inducing more toxins to the body inherent in the drugs themselves.

Furthermore, by eliminating all white sugar and white flour from one's diet, as well as soft drinks, desserts, and bakery products, one's chances of health and longevity are improved. By carefully following a natural, vegetarian diet of organically grown food, the intelligent Wiccan enjoys life to the fullest.

Spiritual

Up to this point we have been discussing the harmful effects of a meat diet on the human body, but we should also consider the ethical and spiritual reasons we, as Wiccans, should abstain from a meat diet as well. All animals have the capacity to learn, remember, love, mourn, rejoice, and suffer just as we humans. As we do not have the capability to restore life, we certainly do not have the right to kill. As the Wiccan Rede so clearly states, every action has its reaction, and every good or evil deed brings forth good or evil fruit threefold!

We humans have come to realize the value of life, human life, that is. There are severe punishments for violent crimes against human beings, yet we extract such cruelty on the animal kingdom without the slightest consideration for those innocent ones who suffer for our greed.

According to the Food and Agriculture Organization, the average number of slaughtered animals in the United States alone is astronomical! On the average, an estimated 229,249,000 cows; 409,500,000 sheep and lambs; 177,296,000 goats; 765,424,000 pigs; 4,032,000 horses; 21,902,400,000 chickens; and 372,300,000 turkeys are murdered every year for their meat. This does not take into account fish and aquatics or the many so-called *game animals* that die every year at the hands of *sportsmen*. If you consider that the total human population of the entire Earth is only a little over five billion, you can clearly see that America alone destroys more lives than Earth's total human population five times over! Is the global suffering that humans are currently experiencing a direct result of the suffering we are inflicting on the animal kingdom? I believe so.

Every diet has its effect on the human mind. We can see this in the animal kingdom as well. Meat-eating animals are often violent in nature, whereas herbivores are more placid and peace loving. Carnivorous animals often kill their young, a trait we rarely, if ever, see in herbivores. Could there be a connection between a meat-centered diet and the atrocities humans extract upon other humans? Could abominable acts, such as murder and abortion, be nullified through the global acceptance of a cruelty-free diet and lifestyle? Perhaps so. The Wiccan Rede is clear on this matter. We, as Wiccans, are free to do as we wish, just as long as *what* we do does not harm another living being.

There are many who claim that a vegetarian diet harms the vegetables we consume and therefore is also in violation of the Rede. This is not entirely true. While it is a proven scientific fact that plants too have a consciousness and can feel some external stimuli, the act of pruning and harvesting actually promotes good health in plants. Of course, when we consume root plants such as carrots and potatoes, we do indeed kill the entire plant. What we must keep in perspective here is the fact that life contains a certain degree of suffering. This must be realized as inevitable. Our job, as Wiccans, is not to eliminate suffering entirely but to alleviate as much of the suffering as we can. This, of course, does not mean shooting the animal with tranquilizers before slaughtering it so as to lessen the pain of its death. It means to cease the killing of noble and innocent creatures merely for greed.

It is true that centuries ago our ancestors hunted for meat and hides. In today's society, where intelligence and technology have replaced ignorant brawn, we do not need meat for food or hides for warmth anymore. As stated above, science has proven that the vegetarian diet is actually healthier for the human being. Knowing this, we can see that opting for a meat diet does not only violate the Wiccan Rede due to the harming of animals, it also violates the Rede because we are harming ourselves!

There are still others, arguing in favor of a meat-based diet, who claim the Gods gave the animals to us for meat. Again, since Wicca is a nature-based religion, we must use our sense of observation to fully address this problem logically. Only after diligent observation can we understand that the animals are not here for *our* food. The purpose of the fish is to maintain clean oceans and waterways, the purpose of chickens and pigs is to keep the land clean, and the purpose of the cow is to give milk. By destroying these wonderful animals we are thereby hindering their true purpose and by doing so, we are committing a heinous ecological crime, thus once again, violating the Wiccan Rede!

Basically, there are three kinds of food: *pure food, stimulating food,* and *impure food.* Milk, butter, fruits, vegetables, and grains fall into the category of pure foods. These are foods that bring calmness to the mind and soothe and nourish the body. Hot spices, meat, alcohol, fish, and eggs are considered stimulating food because they raise the animal passions in humans and bring about a restlessness of mind and body. Needless to say, all food that is rotten, overripe, cured, and putrefied is impure, and thus, can bring only disease and death.

The preference for certain foods is in direct accordance with the evolution of a person's mind. Spiritually and mentally advanced people naturally prefer pure foods to stimulating and impure foods. As a person progresses in mental purity, they normally change from eating a diet of stimulating foods to a diet of pure foods. Seldom do vegetarians revert to eating a lower diet, but non-vegetarians increasingly switch to the higher diet. As a person grows spiritually their desire for meat, alcohol, etc., drastically decreases.

From a purely magickal point of view, a vegetarian diet makes complete sense. Many spellbooks, ancient as well as modern, advise fasting from meat for a few days prior to performing any magickal act. Even my teacher, Raymond Buckland, states not to overindulge in meat before working magick. It is common knowledge that we must be in good physical and spiritual shape to properly work magick successfully, for a sick vine produces poor fruit. Think about this for a moment: *If a short, three-day fast can cleanse our physical and spiritual body from the negative energies associated with a meat diet, thereby granting a higher degree of success to our work, how much more powerful could we become if we abstained from meat altogether?*

I want to close this section by saying this: I am not here to preach to you, only to disclose the facts as I have found them. I have attentively tried to keep my personal biases and opinions out of the discussion and only offer sound scientific evidence to back up my statements. As with all things in Wicca, the ultimate choice is yours.

Summary

In summary, the complete philosophy of the Wicca encompasses five tools to a better spiritual life, namely (1) proper exercise, which aids circulation as well as increases one's magickal energy reserves; (2) proper breathing, which allows for more oxygen absorption; (3) proper relaxation of the body and mind through meditation and relaxation exercises; (4) a natural, vegetarian diet; and (5) proper thinking and concentration of the mind on important spiritual and physical goals (ie: contemplation on the deep philosophical teachings of the Wiccan Rede).

Vitamins

Only living matter contains natural vitamins, and since the physical body cannot manufacture these essential elements, they must be obtained through one's diet. Vitamins are necessary for healthy cell growth and maintenance of our physical body.

Many people believe that vitamin supplementation is the answer to a poorly constructed diet. Some people even think that vitamins can replace food altogether. Sadly enough, there are those who skip entire meals and only take vitamins in hope that they will offset the lack of calories and loss of energy brought on by skipping the meals. The truth is, vitamins cannot be assimilated into one's system without ingesting food. This is one reason why doctors and dieticians recommend taking vitamins with meals rather than on an empty stomach.

Vitamins are necessary for healthy body function because they regulate the metabolism, convert fats and carbohydrates into needed energy, and aid in proper organ and endocrine gland function as well as bone and tissue formation. Vitamins also control the body's use of essential minerals.

Below we will look at the many important vitamins that are required in one's daily diet.

Vitamin A (Beta Carotene)

Vitamin A, or beta carotene, is stored in the subcutaneous fatty tissue of the kidneys and liver. However, these amounts are very minute and an additional supply should be ingested daily through the foodstuffs in one's diet. Foods such as apricots, asparagus, cabbage, carrots, celery, dandelions, lettuce, oranges, parsley, spinach, tomatoes, turnip leaves, and watercress contain ample amounts of beta carotene. The recommended daily requirement of beta carotene is from 5000 to 6000 IU.

Beta carotene aids in proper skin conditioning and healthy vision. It also helps strengthen the immune system, increasing the body's natural ability to fight infection; maintains optimal urinary tract health; and brings vitality to the respiratory system. Vitamin A is essential for proper cell growth.

It is common knowledge that a lack of vitamin A leads to vision problems, but medical problems, such as gall and kidney stones, are the result of a beta carotene deficiency as well.

Vitamin B1 (Thiamin)

Similar to beta carotene, thiamin is also stored in small amounts in the liver and kidneys and should be supplemented daily. Foods that contain ample amounts of thiamin are asparagus, cabbage, carrots, celery, coconuts, dandelions, grapefruits, lemons, parsley, pineapples, pomegranates, radishes, turnip leaves, and watercress. When the dietary intake of carbohydrates are increased, thiamin should be increased as well. The recommended daily requirement of Thiamin is 1.5 milligrams.

Thiamin has a stimulating effect upon the appetite, aids in the proper digestion and absorption of all food materials, promotes healthy cell growth, aids the body's natural resistance to infection, and is essential for proper functioning of nerve tissue. Symptoms of a thiamin deficiency are a slow heartbeat, poor appetite, nervousness, intestinal and gastric problems, poor lactation in females, nerve degeneration, enlargement of the adrenal glands, and a dangerous enlargement of the pancreas.

Vitamin B2 (Riboflavin)

Riboflavin is stored in the body, in greater amounts than thiamin, but its level decreases when levels of minerals and fats increase. Foods that contain ample amounts of riboflavin are apples, apricots, cabbage, carrots, coconuts, dandelions, grapefruits, prunes, spinach, turnip leaves, and watercress. The recommended daily requirement of vitamin B_2 is 1.7 milligrams.

Riboflavin is indispensable for healthy skin and good vision, and is essential for the healthy functioning of the entire gastrointestinal tract. Vitamin B_2 also assists in the absorption of iron into the system and aids protein metabolism. A lack of stamina, many digestive problems, hair loss, cataracts, tongue ulceration, and reduced tissue respiration are some symptoms of a Vitamin B_2 deficiency.

Vitamin C (Ascorbic Acid)

Ascorbic acid is essential for healthy teeth, gums, and bones; it helps heal wounds; repairs scar tissue as well as assists in the mending of fractures; prevents scurvy; builds resistance to infection; aids in the prevention of the common cold; gives strength to the circulatory system; and assists in the assimilation of iron. Vitamin C is absolutely essential for the synthesis of collagen, the intercellular "glue" that holds tissues together. It is also one of the major antioxidant nutrients. Foods that contain ascorbic acid are cucumbers, grapefruits, oranges, papayas, parsley, pineapples, radishes, rhubarb, spinach, tomatoes, turnips, watercress, cabbage, carrots, and asparagus. The recommended daily allowance of vitamin C is 60 milligrams.

Soft and bleeding gums, swollen and painful joints, slow-healing wounds and fractures, bruising, nosebleeds, tooth decay, loss of appetite, muscular weakness, skin hemorrhages, capillary weakness, anemia, and impaired digestion are all visible signs of a Vitamin C deficiency.

Vitamin D

This important nutritional element is not found in fruits, vegetables, or cereals, but is actually the result of ultraviolet irradiation. The recommended daily requirement of Vitamin D is 400 IU.

Vitamin D improves the absorption and utilization of calcium and phosphorous by the body, is required for healthy teeth and bone formation, and is essential for a healthy nervous system and normal heartbeat.

Rickets, tooth decay, the softening of bones, inadequate healing of fractures, lack of stamina, muscular weakness, insufficient calcium assimilation, and a retention of phosphorous in the kidneys are symptoms of a vitamin D deficiency.

Excess amounts of vitamin D in one's system leads to the severe toxicity of vitamin D poisoning. Depression, diarrhea, and abnormal calcium deposits on blood vessel walls, the liver, the kidneys, and the stomach are symptoms of this dangerous malady.

Vitamin E

Vitamin E is a major antioxidant nutrient. It retards cellular aging due to oxidation and supplies oxygen to the blood, which is then carried to the heart and other organs, thus alleviating fatigue. This important nutrient also aids in bringing nourishment to cells, especially in the circulatory system, where it strengthens the capillary walls and guards the red blood cells from destructive poisons. It has also been known to prevent blood clots as well as dissolve calcium deposits in blood vessel walls. Vitamin E has been used by doctors in preventing sterility as well as fighting muscular dystrophy.

Foods that contain this valuable nutrient are celery, lettuce, parsley, spinach, turnip leaves, and watercress. It should be noted that wheat germ is an important source of vitamin E. The recommended daily requirement of vitamin E is 30 to 45 IU.

Vitamin E deficiency may lead to the rupturing of red blood cells, loss of the body's reproductive abilities and various sexually related problems, abnormal intermusculature fat deposits, muscle degeneration, dry skin, hair loss, miscarriages, and sterility in both genders.

I would like to again point out that for the best results one should obtain vitamins through a natural and well-balanced diet. For those who are set on taking over-the-counter vitamin supplementation, there are several types of vitamin E currently available on the market. D-Alpha Tocopherol, which is 100 percent natural, is four times more potent in biological activity than D1-Alpha Tocopherol vitamin E, which is a man-made synthetic. It should also be realized that natural vitamin E is derived from soybeans, whereas synthetic vitamin E is a petroleum by-product.

Minerals

As significant as vitamins are to overall health, they cannot be assimilated into the body without minerals. Another interesting tidbit of information regarding minerals: *While the physical body can manufacture a few important vitamins, it cannot manufacture a single mineral.* This is why a healthy, well-balanced diet containing the proper mineral-enriched foods is so vitally important.

Why are minerals so important to good health? They act as catalysts for many biological reactions within the body, including muscle response, optimal nervous system function, hormone production, proper digestion, and the utilization of nutrients in foods. Furthermore, all tissues and internal fluids contain essential minerals in varying quantities. Minerals are also found in bones, teeth, soft tissue, muscle, blood, and nerve cells; they are vital to overall mental and physical health.

Below is a condensed list of the more important minerals.

Calcium

For the average human subsisting on a meat-based diet, a deficiency in calcium is common, and it is most common in women who have had children. Consuming calcium-rich foods along with exercise is the best means of preventing calcium deficiency. Once calcium is lost and signs of osteopenia develop, the medical problem may be difficult, if not impossible, to reverse. Collapsing of the bones and fractures of the pelvic region may take place in some individuals. A physical shrinking due to age is brought on by vertebral compression fractures caused by osteopenia, normally referred to as *osteoporosis*. Bone density studies can identify patients developing early signs of osteopenia.

Calcium acts as a membrane stabilizer, strengthening cell walls, and natural tranquilizer, as do magnesium and potassium. Foods rich in calcium are grapefruits, cranberries, spinach, cheese, watercress, figs, oranges, turnips, carrots, cabbage, milk, blackberries, and rhubarb. Persons wishing to supplement their diets with calcium in tablet or pill form should know that for best results calcium should be taken with magnesium in a ratio of 2 : 1. The recommended daily allowance of calcium is 1000 to 1500 milligrams. A calcium/magnesium supplement may be taken at bedtime to promote sleep.

Iron

The major purpose of iron is to combine with protein and copper to make hemoglobin. Hemoglobin carries oxygen in the blood from the lungs to the tissues that need it to maintain basic life functions. Iron increases the quality of the blood and enhances the body's ability to resist stress and disease. Iron is also necessary for the formation of myoglobin, which is found only in muscle tissue and supplies oxygen to muscle cells for use in the chemical reaction that results in muscle contraction. Iron also prevents fatigue and promotes good skin tone.

The symptoms of iron deficiency are muscle weakness, paleness of skin, constipation, and anemia.

Foods rich in iron are beans, peas, whole wheat, oatmeal, prunes, spinach, cheese, dates, watercress, raisins, oranges, turnips, tomatoes, bananas, carrots, and cabbage. The recommended daily allowance of iron is 18 milligrams.

Copper

Copper is necessary for the assimilation and utilization of iron in the body. It also aids in the oxidation of ascorbic acid, and combines with ascorbic acid to form elastin. Copper also assists with proper bone and red blood cell formation.

The symptoms of a copper deficiency are general weakness, impaired respiration, and skin ulcerations.

Dried as well as fresh fruits and all green leafy vegetables are a prime source of copper. The exact daily requirements of copper have not yet been established.

Iodine

Iodine regulates the body's production of energy, stimulates the basic metabolic rate, and assists in the development and proper function of the thyroid gland. Overall mental health, correct articulation of speech, and healthy hair, skin, and teeth are reliant upon a properly functioning thyroid gland.

The symptoms of an iodine deficiency are an enlarged thyroid gland, slow mental reactions, dry skin and hair, excessive weight gain, and loss of physical and mental vigor.

The best sources for iodine are kelp and sea lettuce. Other iodine-rich foods are asparagus, cabbage, carrots, cranberries, cucumbers, pineapples, prunes, radishes, spinach, tomatoes, and watercress.

The recommended daily allowance of iodine is 150 micrograms.

Potassium

Potassium is essential for proper function of every cell in the body. Potassium works with sodium to regulate a correct waste balance in the body, as well as normalizing heart rhythm. This vital mineral also preserves the alkalinity of body fluids, aids in reducing high blood pressure, sends oxygen to the brain that is required for normal mental operation, and promotes healthy skin.

Symptoms of a potassium deficiency are poor reflexes, various nervous disorders, muscle damage, respiratory failure, and cardiac arrest.

All fruits and vegetables are rich in potassium and should be consumed on a daily basis since a recommended daily allowance has not yet been universally established.

Magnesium

Magnesium is vital for the regulation of cardiac neuromuscular activity and calcium and ascorbic acid metabolism, and conversion of blood sugar into energy.

Symptoms of a magnesium deficiency are calcium depletion in the body, heart spasms and cardiac arrhythmia, increased nervousness, muscular excitability or spasm, mental confusion, and kidney stones.

Most foods contain ample amounts of magnesium. Common sources are almonds, cashews, nuts, peanuts, lima beans, whole wheat, brown rice, oatmeal, dates, raisins, spinach, and most fruits and vegetables.

The recommended daily allowance of magnesium is 1 to 2 milligrams.

∽

Required Reading for This Chapter

Hunter, Jennifer. *21st Century Wicca: A Young Witch's Guide to Living the Magickal Life*. Citadel Press, 1997.

K. Amber. *True Magick: A Beginner's Guide*. Llewellyn, 1990.

∽

3

THE CIRCLE

THE THIRD COUPLET of the Wiccan Rede teaches: "*Cast the circle thrice about, to keep unwelcomed spirits out.*" It is in this lesson that the Wiccan Rede first teaches us about the basic fundamentals of magick and the supernatural. This couplet also directly relates to the sixth couplet of the poem: "*Deosil go by waxing moon, chanting out the Seax-Wiccan Runes,*" as well as the seventh couplet: "*Widdershins go by waning moon, chanting out the baneful tune.*"

For centuries, circles have been used as symbols of protection, as well as being practical protection devices in and of themselves. Witches and pagans may have been the first people to use circles as tools of protection, but certainly, we have not been the only people to use them. As far back as Sumerian and Babylonian times, physicians and nurses drew circles around the beds of the infirm to protect the sick from demons and devils. Jews and Germans in the Middle Ages would likewise inscribe circles around women in labor to protect them, and their unborn child, from various evil spirits. Even non-pagan, monotheistic religions used circles. Catholic bishops and popes, when in battle during the crusades, would often draw an invisible circle of protection around themselves with their staff, as a supernatural means of protection.

Circles have also been used in the building of religious structures and monoliths, such as the world-famous Stonehenge. Lesser-known sites, like dolmen stones and fairy rings, also abound and many are still in existence today, especially in Britain, Scotland, and Ireland.

What makes the circle so enticing and useful in connection to its protective properties? One glance at the circle itself reveals the answer: *A circle is eternal, without beginning or end.* And herein lies its supernatural strength and potential.

Another thing to keep in mind is the dual nature of the circle itself. Circles are not only constructed to keep negativity out, but are also designed to contain the intense supernatural energy raised during magickal ritual. The first thing the working witch does prior to ritual is *cast the circle*. Once the circle is cast, and as the Wiccan Rede teaches, it must be cast *thrice about*, then the witch can safely begin the magickal ritual at hand. During the ritual, enormous amounts of supernatural energy are raised and directed to its cause. When the energy is released and sent on its way to the target, the ritual spellworking is completed. Then and only then can the circle be broken.

So what does it mean to "*cast the circle thrice about*"? It simply means that in order to construct the strongest possible circle, three things should be executed in its building. First, with your athame or magickal sword, you should inscribe the actual circle. Second, you should banish all unseen negative energies from the circle using salted water. And third, you should further reinforce the protective properties of the circle by fuming its boundaries with the proper incense.

One thing to remember: There are no hard and fast rules when casting a circle, so long as the three basic fundamentals are always adhered to. In the following pages, I will explain the way I personally construct my magickal circle for ritual work as well as Sabbat and Esbat celebrations. Again, this is simply *my* method, and has worked well for me for over the past decade. It is not the *only* way to build a circle, so feel free to improvise your own circle construction if you don't feel comfortable with this method.

Building the Circle

In order to set the atmosphere and attune my mind to the task at hand, I first recite this short prayer:

"My dear Lord and Lady,[1] *I humbly ask you both to join me this night as I come before you in love. I come to worship you and to partake in living the Wiccan mysteries. May I always live my life in your service and in accordance to your Will. So mote it be."*

Now, take the athame or magickal sword and slowly walk the entire circumference of the circle, beginning at the northern corner[2] and proceeding to the eastern corner, then to the southern corner, on to the western corner, and finally closing the circle once again in the north. Keep the blade pointed down and focus your complete and undivided attention on what you are doing, which is infusing your psychic energy into the circle's boundary. If necessary, visualize your psychic and magickal energies traveling from your body's center, down your arms, and into the hilt of your magickal weapon, then traversing down the length of its

---

[1] If you have already chosen a personal deity, such as Woden, Freya, Isis, or Ra, feel free to insert their names here. To make the prayer even more intimate, you could call on the Lord and Lady as your eternal parents by using the wording, "dear eternal mother, dear eternal father." Again, the choice is yours; do what feels right.

[2] Some traditions of Wicca begin circle construction in the eastern corner of the circle, to give prime reverence to the rising Sun God. Since my chosen tradition of Wicca is a northern Teutonic one, I prefer to begin my circle construction in the north. As usual, the choice is yours.

blade and finally jumping from its point in a bright blue electric arc of power directly into the circle itself.

Next, take up the bowl of salted water, which incidentally should have been blessed for this special occasion, and begin the blessing of the circle. Again, begin at the northern corner of the circle and travel around its boundary in the same manner as you did with the sword.

Sprinkle a few drops of blessed water in the north corner of the circle while saying:

"By the strength of this blessed water I now consecrate this circle and hereby invite all the good spirits of the north to guard this holy gate!"

Now walk to the east corner and sprinkle a few drops of blessed water in the east corner of the circle while saying:

"By the strength of this blessed water I now consecrate this circle and hereby invite all the good spirits of the east to guard this holy gate!"

Now walk to the south corner and sprinkle a few drops of blessed water in the south corner of the circle while saying:

"By the strength of this blessed water I now consecrate this circle and hereby invite all the good spirits of the south to guard this holy gate!"

Now walk to the west corner and sprinkle a few drops of blessed water in the west corner of the circle while saying:

"By the strength of this blessed water I now consecrate this circle and hereby invite all the good spirits of the west to guard this holy gate!"

Lastly, take up the censor and incense, which also should have been blessed for this special occasion, and begin the fuming of the circle. Once again, begin at the northern corner of the circle and travel around its boundary in the same manner as you did with the sword and the blessed water.

With the censor and incense, fume the north corner of the circle while saying:

"By the strength of this holy incense, I now purify this circle and hereby invite all the good spirits of the north to guard this holy gate!"

Proceed eastward and fume the east corner of the circle while saying:

"By the strength of this holy incense, I now purify this circle and hereby invite all the good spirits of the east to guard this holy gate!"

Proceed southward and fume the south corner of the circle while saying:

"By the strength of this holy incense, I now purify this circle and hereby invite all the good spirits of the south to guard this holy gate!"

Proceed westward and fume the west corner of the circle while saying:

"By the strength of this holy incense, I now purify this circle and hereby invite all the good spirits of the west to guard this holy gate!"

After the circle is built you are then ready to proceed with your ritual, spellworking, or Sabbat or Esbat celebration, knowing full well that you are safe within its holy boundaries.

Breaking the Circle

At the close of your ritual, always break the circle prior to leaving its boundary. This is simply done by taking your athame or sword and cutting the circle open. I personally use a waist-high, horizontal cut, and slice the air in a circular pattern, in the same direction in which it was built: North, east, south, and west. While making the cut, simply recite these words:

"This ritual is now over and the circle is now broken. I thank the Gods and all the good spirits that participated with me in my ritual. Go in peace and return in peace. Blessed be!"

A Simple Circle Spell of Protection

If you are in dire need of protection, yet don't have ample time to cast a full circle and perform an entire ritual, then do this simple circle spell of protection. Simply spin sun-wise[3] three times while chanting the following words:

> *"By the power of three times three, may this circle bring protection to me!"*

Blessing the Salted Water

Hold both hands over the bowl of salted water, palms down and hands open, and infuse the liquid with your magickal psychic energy while saying:

> *"Salt is life and water is life. By the power of the Gods, I hereby bless this salted water that it shall drive out all negative energies and entities wherever it is sprinkled."*

Blessing the Holy Incense

Place the lit charcoal in the censor and sprinkle a few grains of incense upon it. As the fragrant smoke begins to rise, hold both hands over the censor, palms down

---

[3] Clockwise (ie: *Deosil*).

and hands open, and infuse the incense with your magickal psychic energy. Recite these words:

"Incense is a gift from the Gods, and by the power of the Gods, I hereby bless this holy incense so it shall purify and drive out all negative energies and entities wherever it is burned."

A Guided Meditation for Gaining Wisdom

Once you feel that your skills at building the circle are adequate, you will most likely wish to begin your magickal ritual and spellworkings. Guided meditations are also an excellent way to gain intimate knowledge of the universe. Following is a guided meditation for gaining spiritual wisdom. Once again, there are no hard and fast rules for guided meditations. If you so wish, and I encourage you to do so, please feel free to use your own creativity and write your own.

Introduction to Guided Meditations

In its most simplistic form, the guided meditation is simply a story that your mind will follow during meditation. For best results, record the meditation story in your own voice on a tape machine, then as you listen, simply allow your mind to wander through the many amazing worlds and experience their myriad wonders. Your mind should follow the meditation as recorded, but always remember that intuition is more important than any written word. Go with your gut instinct and listen to the Gods themselves, for they are the *real* teachers here!

The goal of this meditation is to put yourself in a trance, thus allowing the mind to wander the astral plane and extract hidden wisdom.

There is no need for elaborate trappings such as incense, candles, robes, etc. This is an *inner journey* and you should focus on that. If you feel that the above-mentioned paraphernalia will help you get into a trance-like state more easily, then by all means, use them. Just be sure that they do not become a crutch, thus limiting your overall progress and ultimate potential.

This is only one meditation—you can devise many others using this one as a guide. Prior to beginning your meditation, decide upon a goal and structure the meditation accordingly. This meditation is merely a foundation upon which all others can be built. There are certain places where this meditation will take you, and certain things that will happen. Do not worry if your mind goes wandering off and does not follow the exact guidelines of the meditation. Actually, this is what the meditation is designed to do!

You will see many strange images and hear many strange sounds; you will meet many strange entities and experience many strange emotions. Just relax and go with it. Extracting the secrets of the ages is not easy and Wicca is not intended to be a walk in the park. Wisdom is won only through diligent effort. Keep this in mind when treading this path.

Please note that this meditation is of the Seax-Wiccan tradition of Wicca. As stated earlier, there are many traditions within our gentle faith. This is simply one. Look at it like the many spokes of a bicycle wheel; many paths leading to the same center . . . the same goal. It is to your benefit to examine and explore many different traditions of Wicca until you find one that suits you.

Preparation

Cast your circle as described above. Sit in the center of your circle and face south. Take a deep, full breath and hold it for a second or two, then exhale slowly. Once you have expended your breath, relax into your seated posture and, with eyes closed, listen to the guided meditation.

The Quest for Spiritual Wisdom

I am relaxed, totally relaxed. I can feel the energies of my body and soul mingling and surging through one another. Even though my physical eyes are closed, I can see shapes and colors before me. I feel my soul separate from my physical body, yet I remain ever conscious of my physical attributes.

Slowly I stand and look around. I can see the circle glowing all about me, pulsating with the energy of the ages. In the south area of the circle, I can see a mist building. The fog is getting thicker and more opaque, and I can smell a faint mustiness lingering in the air. I walk toward the thick layers of mist and the fog parts before me. Suddenly I come to a large gate. Carefully I reach out, and my hands encounter the aged wood of that ancient portal and the rusted iron bands that fasten it to immense hinges. Inset directly in the center of the gate is a heavy iron plaque, and on that plaque, the Wiccan pentagram is deeply engraved.

In my ears, I can hear the ringing vibration of the universe. Suddenly, and without warning, the gate begins to open. As the door slowly swings wide, unassisted by me, a brilliant white light enters in over the threshold and singes my eyes. I stand in utter amazement for a moment or two, letting my eyes adjust to the intensity of the light. Cautiously, I walk through the gate.

I take a few steps through the gate, gazing in awe at the magnificent landscape surrounding me, and then I pause and turn to look back through the gate. I can see my physical body, still sitting inside my circle, silently meditating. In a blink of an eye, the gate swings shut and I am alone.

I feel a cold rush of anxiety pour over my being, yet it vanishes as quickly as it came. I turn and continue walking south, seeking to explore the wondrous landscape before me.

All about me are the greenest pastures that I have ever seen. The bright sun is shining with an intensity I have never before experienced, and the skies are the deepest blue that my imagination has ever beheld. Far off in the distance I notice a thick forest with tall dark trees, and while the atmosphere is beyond beauty, I cannot help but feel a deep emotion of despair welling up inside me.

All of a sudden, I hear the sound of many hooves beating the earth and the panting breath of a heavy horse. From behind me comes a rider, and as I turn to gaze at that proud warrior, I see his breast streaked in crimson red. A lone wolf howls as witchcraft's father rides past me like the wind; Sleipnir's eight steel-shod hooves thundering loudly as they go their way. Deafening moans the earth as Woden rides to Helheim's lofty hall.

For a moment, I stand in amazement as I watch the

rider vanish before my eyes into the distant forest, before once again taking up my journey and proceeding southward.

Onward I walk through this lush pasture, as wide as the horizon and extending as far as my eyes can see. Yet, in the far distance, I espy the dark forest beyond the pasture's boundary, and towering over even the mightiest of trees is the lone Ash where my destination lies. Ever green, it stands beside the *Norn's* spring, a tall tree that throws from its boughs sparkling drops of clear dew down into the valley below.

(Pause for a few moments in the narration at this point and allow yourself the luxury to explore the pasture and the outer limits of the dark forest. Take in all the sights, sounds, and smells of your surroundings. Utilize your complete senses when experiencing this realm, and also note any emotional and mental feelings you have during this time.)

After some time, I notice the sky has darkened and a strange chilling wind is gently blowing up from the south. As I continue on my journey, far off in the distance, I notice a lone herdsman tending his flock. He is old, yet stout, with a long gray beard and a worn and tattered cloak of the strangest hue of blue. A wide-brimmed hat is pulled down over his right eye concealing his aged face.

"Hail to thee, stranger," I shout, as I wave my hand in friendship, yet the old man pauses and leans heavily on his staff.

"Only a fool would linger here," he yells with a roar, "to wander through the shadows of night. Can you not see that the graves gape open and fires are rising? You have no business here . . . make haste!"

A terrible anxiety rushes over me at the doom of his heavy words, and I stagger past the old man, diligent to extract the riddle of this realm, and continue southward on my journey. After a few steps, I pause and turn around, but to my amazement, the herdsman and his flock are nowhere to be seen.

I notice the sun beginning to sink low on the horizon, and am filled with a feeling of intense calmness, and even though it is clearly summer, an almost bitter cold rushes up from the ground into my very being. Onward I walk, pursuing my quest, even at the price of my own doom, and I finally enter the dark forest.

A few paces into that cold and foreboding forest, I notice that the flora and fauna have changed considerably. Nowhere do I see any plant that is recognizable; and the canopy overhead is so thick and entangled that not even a shard of sunlight penetrates to the forest floor. Finally, I come to a great clearing in the forest where I find a huge barrow mound. A thick fog begins to send out its icy tendrils, and all about me a heavy sent of muskiness hangs on the air. Suddenly, there arises a great flame, it roars high above the barrow mound, and the earth shakes beneath my feet. The grave opens and mighty *Angantyr* appears before me.

Fierce is his gaze, and fiercer yet are his stern words. He is clothed in the armaments of a warrior king, with a great oaken shield and a long sword, wet with blood. Like a clap of thunder his words roar, and my heart weakens as he speaks.

"The gate of Helheim is down," he says. "The graves are open and a great flame flickers over the land. Awesome it is to gaze upon it. Don't stay here, make haste while you still can!" And with those final words of warning, he vanishes in a waft of smoke, as does the entire clearing.

Once again, I am alone with my thoughts in the center of the great dark forest; no barrow mound can be seen, no heavy scent of musk can be smelled. The great flame is gone and I am alone. I come to a large Oak, and sit at its base.

(Once again, pause in the narration, and listen intensely to the wisdom of the forest. After a considerable amount of time, perhaps only a few minutes, resume the guided tale and continue on your journey.)

Rising from my seat at the base of the Oak, I continue on the journey, stumbling through the forest in darkness. After much wandering, I come to a black stream laden with muck and thick sludge. A pungent stench fills my lungs and I cover my face with a rag. To my right, I hear splashing, and crouch in the ferns to conceal myself. Through the dense weeds I see men wading through the heavy stream. Oath breakers they were, yet others had murdered. How I know these things, I know not, yet know them I do! Some had lured another man's love and basked in the pleasures of adultery, and there the serpent sucked on corpses and the wolves rent dead men's flesh.

On my hands and knees, I crawl through decaying earth to a clearing in the forest, and there I gaze in amazement, for the black stream is no longer black, but a deep turquoise blue. And in the stream is swimming a great fish, yet he is the color of a man's flesh, and no gills are to be seen anywhere on his body.

"My name is *Andvari*," the great fish says as he peers at me though unblinking eyes. "Woden is my father, yet long ago a Norn fixed my fate to spend my life swimming." With those few words he leaps from the waters and disappears in a great shower of waves.

I test the waters and cross the stream; its wetness burns at my flesh and singes my lungs. In my mind's eye, I see a soot-red cock in the halls of Helheim, and know my fate is near. I continue on and many strange sights do I see. Finally I come to the base of the Ash, its nine roots wound about a dark and foreboding cave.

Garm moans loudly from Gnipa cave, yet his rope will one day break and he will run free! Many spells have I learned and I clearly see the doom that awaits the Gods!

I enter the cave and find a stair going down and down and down. Into the womb of the Earth I walk, feeling my way through the darkness by only touch of hand. The walls are wet with slime, and the stillness of the air is addictive. I must fight the urge to abandon my quest, for I feel tired and in need of rest. Helheim is upon me, and its icy grip enthralls me, yet my strength prevails and I continue.

At the bottom of the stair is a chamber that opens to an immense space; at the south end of the chamber, far from sunlight, stands a hall. On the shores of the dead that hall stands, its main door facing north. From its roof drips deadly poison, and the rooms writhe with twisting snakes! In that hall live three maidens wise in lore, from Jotunheim they came, but now reside here in this dark hall. One is called *Urd*, another is *Verdandi*, and *Skuld* is the third. They carve out runes and establish the laws that decide the lives men are to lead; this is how they mark out humanity's fate.

Cautiously, I enter the hall and see a well at its center. Apprehensively, I approach the well and gaze into its still waters. The face of the dark wanderer stares back at me, yet I am not approached by the Norns.

Now I can say where *Heimdall's* horn lies hidden! Beneath this holy tree that hides the sun, a waterfall keeps the branches cool as water flows from Woden's eye!

There I sit alone beneath that ancient well, until at last, the old one comes. The lord of the Aesir he is, and gravely he looks into my face.

"Why have you come here," he asks, "and what would you ask me?"

(Pause from the narrative for a moment. Feel free to ask your question, yet listen diligently to the words of All-father, and a great rune will be revealed to you.)

"Now I know, Woden, how you lost your eye, for it lies in the base at Mimir's well. Every morning Mim drinks wisdom from your tribute, and I shall remember your teachings from this day forward."

And as I speak these words, I rise from the well and stumble across the hall to where a large throne stands. There, at the base of that throne do I sit and take rest, for in my heart, I will sing from the sage's chair, near the Norn's sacred spring. Here will I contemplate the words of the wise when they speak of hidden runes.

Yet, Woden again rises from the depths of my mind and speaks unto me! "Far have I traveled," he says, "and many things have I tried. Against the gods have I proved my strength, yet do you wish to know what words of power I whispered in my son's ear when he laid upon the Pyre?"

(Again, pause with the narration and listen for a deep teaching.)

After some time, the stillness of Helheim begins to permeate me and I realize that I must go. I see a raven soaring through airless skies and an eight-hoofed steed thunders forth; suddenly I am spirited through a vast darkness and over black pastures. I see the flames licking at the heels of the dead, yet a chilling calm engulfs me.

Soon I see the gate, its door gaping open, and my physical body sitting there waiting for my return. I enter my body, yet I remember Sigurd's words: "Every warrior enjoys his wealth until one destined day. Sooner or later each man surrenders all that he has to Helheim."

I take a deep breath and open my eyes. I have returned!

(Thus ends your guided meditation. Sit for a few minutes to relax and absorb any important spiritual information before

breaking the circle. Soon after breaking the circle, write down all imperative thoughts and emotions in your journal so that you do not forget them.)

Required Reading for This Chapter

Coleman, Martin. *Communing with the Spirits.* Samuel Weiser, 1998.

Cunningham, Scott. *Living Wicca.* Llewellyn, 1993.

Laurie, Erynn Rowan. *A Circle of Stones.* Eschaton, 1995.

4

RHYMING SPELLS

THE FOURTH COUPLET of the Wiccan Rede teaches: "*To bind the spell well every time, let the spell be spoken in rhyme.*" Here, the main lesson is that of the magic of enchantments and incantations. These are spoken spells, so vividly powerful that the caster's mind is fused with the magickal energy being weaved, and hence, no other prop or tool is needed for the result to manifest. Of course, other magickal implements[1] can be employed during these enchantments for added strength, but in a pinch, the spoken word is enough to cause immediate and lasting results.

The phrase *"To bind the spell well every time, let the spell be spoken in rhyme,"* leads us back to ancient times, when witches and pagans cast their enchantments and sang their incantations by way of rhyming the magickal words of power. This was done for one simple reason:

[1] Please see below for enchantment examples, with and without magickal paraphernalia.

Rhymes are easy for the mind to remember. Sure, there are many incantations and enchantments that do not make use of rhyme, such as *Sasnakra Thar Thar Thamaru Mommon Betos Opranu*,[2] and *Anail Nathrock Uthvass Bethudd Dochiel Diende*,[3] and they can and do work as well as any rhyming spell. However, it is just easier to memorize enchantments that rhyme.

One key factor in making a charm work is concentration; therefore, memorization is of the utmost importance. If you fumble with the words, or simply cannot remember their order, it is much more difficult to concentrate on the spell and its desired result. Also, while enchantments in foreign tongues are quite exotic, and they do have the tendency to add to the magickal atmosphere of the moment, there is something to be said for casting in one's own language. If you cast a rhyming incantation in your own tongue, you will not only have an easy time memorizing the spell but you will also fully comprehend its meaning. Understanding the words and knowing their complete definitions is as important as remembering the order of the words themselves. Even if you are able to memorize foreign

---

[2] The *Spell of Summoning* is an enchantment of the author's own design.

[3] The ancient *Celtic Charm of Making: The 21 Lessons of Merlyn,* Douglas Monroe, Llewellyn, 1998.

words and enchantments, if you do not fully grasp their inherent meaning, most likely the spell will not work; at worst, it may backfire and manifest the exact opposite result to your desire!

Today there is a fad in the New Age and occult publishing industry—Spellbooks. There seem to be tens of thousands, if not hundreds of thousands, of spellbooks floating around. New Age and occult book publishers spend millions of dollars churning out these tomes yearly to fill the demand put on them by neophyte magicians, witches, and pagans. For some reason, many people today feel that a spell or incantation is more powerful if it was created by someone else rather than themselves. This is simply not the case. When you have a strong need or desire, that need and desire is extremely personal. If you pour every ounce of energy into designing an enchantment for your specific purpose, you increase the overall potential for the spell's success. The old saying holds true here—*if you want something done right, it is best to do it yourself.* I firmly believe this, especially where crafting enchantments is concerned.

A good rule of thumb when crafting your own enchantment is to keep the incantation short and to the point. Long, drawn-out incantations are simply overkill. It is much better to construct a short phrase, and then repeat it a certain number of times. For instance, the numbers three, six, and nine are powerful numbers and are used often in witchcraft. Design a short incantation for your specific need and then simply chant it over and over, three, six, or nine times. It is easy as that!

To get you started, I have provided a few all-purpose spells. Please feel free to redesign them to fit your own specific needs. Also, be sure to keep a magickal journal so that you can keep track of your spell's success ratio.

When you craft a new enchantment, write it down in your magickal journal, and then list the date you cast it (every time you cast it). Be sure to write down your desired result as well, so that you do not forget the reason you cast the spell! When the charm manifests, write down the date that it manifested and also make a note of how many days it took to manifest. If, after a week or two, the charm does not seem to be working, simply go back and re-evaluate the enchantment, making any changes you feel might add to its strength and success, then cast it again. Keeping track of your spell's success ratio in this manner, you will become intimate with your own magickal abilities and develop your overall psychic intuition. By constantly monitoring your enchantments, and altering them if need be, you will gain the desired insight into the actual workings of your own magickal powers. This is the fascinating area where magick actually becomes science! The difference between a neophyte and an adept is this: *The neophyte uses spells that others create; the adept creates spells from scratch!* By studying all you can about spell crafting and working diligently to master the art of creating enchantments, you will be well on your way to becoming an adept.

Examples of Enchantments Without Paraphernalia

Enchantment for Love

"By the power of nine times nine[4] let true love be mine!" (Repeat the chant nine times.)

Enchantment for Health

"Magickal powers of earth, air, fire, and sea,[5] destroy this illness and bring health back to me!"

---

[4]The power of numbers is much used in magick and witchcraft. Nine is believed to be the most powerful number by many traditions. The formula of nine multiplied by nine is exceedingly powerful because the end result can be reduced to a single digit and once again becomes nine. (Example: $9 \times 9 = 81 = 8 + 1 = 9$)

[5]This enchantment makes use of the four elements: earth, air, fire, and water.

Enchantment for Money

"By the ancient forces of old, bring me money and wealth untold! MONEY!" (Repeat three, six, or nine times, while spinning deosil the same number of times that the enchantment is spoken. With each revolution, spin faster and chant louder, until the desired number is reached, then scream the word *money* at the top of your lungs and fall to the ground. Remain on the ground until your breathing and heart rate return to normal, to be sure that all the magickal energy you raised has been successfully released.)

Enchantment for Success

"By the strength of three times nine,[6] allow this success to be mine!"

Enchantment for Strength[7]

"Silver rays flowing, Full Moon's power growing; coming, going, coming, going, flowing down on me! Moonbeams flow-

---

[6] Again, we see the magickal formula surrounding the number nine by way of the following formula ($3 \times 9 = 27 = 2 + 7 = 9$). By utilizing the power of numbers in your enchantments, you will add to their overall strength, thus guaranteeing a higher degree of success in your magickal workings.

[7] Ventimiglia, Mark. *The Wiccan Prayer Book.* Citadel Press, 2000.

ing, Goddess power growing; coming, going, coming, going, flowing into me!"

Enchantment for Protection

"Mother Goddess, hear my plea, bless me, guard me, protect me!"

Enchantment for Happiness

"From dark to light, the spell goes forth, to cross the void of space and time. From misery to happiness, the power returns to me and mine." (Chant this incantation in a joyful manner to destroy depression and melancholy. Recite nine times and the spell is done.)

Enchantment for Prophetic Dreams

"Divine Mother, you who was, is, and forever shall be, please grant prophetic dreams to me. Divine Father, you who created everything we see, please bring visions of the future to me." (While lying in your bed, repeat this enchantment over and over until you fall asleep.)

Enchantment for Rain[8]

"Goddess bring the rain down, giving life to the ground; energy to feed the seed, Mother Nature's gift to me. God bring the

[8] Ibid.

rain down, giving life to the ground; energy to feed the seed and a healthy harvest bring!"

Examples of Enchantments With Paraphernalia

Enchantment to Cure a Headache

Tie a blue strand of yarn around your neck before you retire for the evening. Upon waking in the morning, go to a park or some other wooded place and remove the yarn from your neck. Be sure not to break the circle of yarn when removing it. Then loosely tie the piece of yarn to the limb of an oak tree while saying: *"King of the forest, oh mighty Oak tree, please remove this headache from me!"* Be sure to leave a few coins at the base of the tree as a token of your thanks.

Enchantment to Raise a Storm

Take a few pinches of ground mistletoe in your right hand[9] and go outside. Face north and say in a loud and clear voice: *"By the strength of mighty Thor, bring a storm, let thunder roar!"* Open your hand and in one strong breath, blow the mistletoe to the sky. The spell is cast.[10]

[9] If you are left handed, hold the herb in your left hand.
[10] Please see Chapter Nine of this manual for wind magick, and Chapter Ten for herbal magick.

Enchantment to Get a Better Job

Obtain a three-foot[11] piece of hemp rope that is about the diameter of your little finger. Begin the spell by tying knots in the rope. Recite a line of this enchantment for every knot you tie. To complete the spell and release its magickal energy simply toss the rope into a fire when all the knots have been tied. "*Through knot of one, my spell has begun. Through knot of two, it will come true. Through knot of three, my power shall be. Through knot of four, this power I store. Through knot of five, my magick is alive. Through knot of six, a job I will fix. Through knot of seven, I draw power from heaven. Through knot of eight, I open the gate. By knot of nine, this job is mine!*"

Enchantment to Pass a Test

When you sit down to take a test, simply trace a pentagram[12] with your index finger at the top of your test paper while saying: "*I send this charm for the Wights to see, give me aid and wisdom bring!*"

---

[11] Once again numerology plays an important part in magick, as we see by the formula used here: (3 feet = 36 inches = 36 = 3 + 6 = 9).

[12] Please see Chapter Seventeen for more information concerning pentagrams.

Enchantment to Charge a Talisman with Power

Lay the chosen talisman on your altar between two white candles. Place your hands over the talisman, palms down. Recite this enchantment: *"By the power of sun and moon, charge this talisman, guard me from doom. By the power of moon and sun, charge this talisman, this spell is done!"*

Leave the talisman on your altar until both white candles have burned themselves out.

Required Reading for This Chapter

Buckland, Raymond. *Buckland's Complete Book of Witchcraft*. Llewellyn, 1986.

Cunningham, Scott. *Earth Power*. Llewellyn, 1983.

Dunwich, Gerina. *Everyday Wicca*. Citadel Press, 1997.

5

THE QUALITIES
OF THE STUDENT

THE FIFTH COUPLET of the Wiccan Rede teaches: "*Soft of eye an' light of touch, speak ye little an' listen much*." With this phrase we can see that the Wiccan Rede does much more than just teach us about religion and magick, for this lesson rings clear with the wisdom of common sense and the practical instruction of dealing with others in a mature and civilized manner.

Many problems in today's society are the result of not enough listening. From domestic squabbles to major international wars, we can see both sides squaring off, screaming at the top of their lungs, and making no effort to seriously cooperate to resolve the issues at hand. If the majority of the population would heed this simple instruction and "*speak ye little an' listen much*," a large amount of suffering would be alleviated and most of the world's problems would disappear.

Also, remembering that Wicca is a nature-oriented

religion, we can see how observing nature is an intricate part of practicing one's faith. "*Soft of eye an' light of touch*" guides us to the gentle practice of observing nature and one's surroundings. When visiting a secluded wooded location, we should pass by as a shade in the night, observing yet not disturbing those that inhabit the area. If we walk along a lonely beach, the same instruction holds true; we should leave not a trace of our being there, save for footprints in the sand.

When we cultivate the ability to silently observe and listen to what nature has to teach, the doors of enlightenment are opened wide and true wisdom and knowledge is obtained. However, for true enlightenment to be gained, we must first eliminate any preconceived notions and prejudices we may have about a great many things. Once this is mastered, we will then be able to see the world as it really is, in all its beauty and glory. Then, and only then, will the greater scheme of things be fully understood. This is the true essence of Wicca, as well as all nature-oriented, earth-based systems of spirituality—to totally comprehend one's place in the world and become *one with nature*.

A Simple Listening Exercise

This exercise can be modified to suit your individual needs. For best results, one should execute this exercise at least once a month.

Go to a secluded location. It should be out of doors, preferably a quiet wood, lonely beach, empty field, or isolated mountaintop. Take a slow-paced walk, in silence, and simply *look and listen* to your surroundings. Take in all the sights, smells, and sounds of the entire area. Feel the warm sun on your face, or perhaps the cool drizzle on your cheek; experience the hot sand between your toes, or the frigid cold arctic blasts upon your back. Make mental notes of the emotions and impressions you receive during these simple walks.

To give you a better overall perspective of nature, it is best to perform this exercise under many different weather conditions, as well as in many diverse locations.

It is extremely important to listen and not speak during this exercise. The Goddess and God are aware of you; They know the reason why you are there. You need not invoke Them, or even recite a prayer. Just be there and give Them your full attention. Do not let the effortlessness of this exercise fool you; the benefits gained far outweigh its simplicity.

༄

Required Reading for This Chapter

Harner, Michael. *The Way of the Shaman*. Harper & Row, 1981.
Rogers, Spencer. *The Shaman's Healing Way*. Acoma Books, 1976.

6

THE RUNES

Disclaimer

THROUGHOUT THIS BOOK, where the runes are concerned, I have used the early runic works of Dr. Edred Thorsson as general research material. Even though Dr. Thorsson's work has provided the catalyst for deep thought, it is my understanding that his current involvement with satanic organizations such as the Temple of Set and the Order of Knights of the Trapezoid has clouded his thinking and inadvertently taken his research down a wrongful and murky path. Satanism is supported by the philosophic beliefs of those who wish to rebel against Christianity, for Satan himself is a Christian invention, and Satanism has no place in witchcraft or European paganism!

For many years the public has looked at Dr. Thorsson as the foremost authority on Germanic lore and runology, but my recent findings have uncovered evidence that his teachings are contrary to authentic Teutonic culture and spiritual beliefs. In much of his theories he disregards sacred Teutonic philosophical and numerical values in favor of the Kabbalistic philosophies of the ancient Middle East. There is even some proof in his most recent works that he has borrowed alien ideas and concepts from the Orient as well.

This book may be considered highly controversial, since it contradicts the established teachings of Dr. Thorsson. While I respect Dr. Thorsson's scholarly approach to research, I cannot accept the concept of allowing foreign ideas such as Kabbalistic philosophy and Satanism to infiltrate the sacred teachings of runology. I believe an intelligent and educated public will understand my views on this matter and hopefully, in time, come to agree with me.

This being said, let it be known that I have no affiliation with the Temple of Set or the Order of Knights of the Trapezoid, nor do I have any affiliation with Dr. Thorsson or any of his colleagues.

—Mark Ventimiglia
Wood River, Illinois
October 10, 2002

The sixth and seventh couplets of the Wiccan Rede teach: *"Deosil go by waxing moon, chanting out the Seax-Wiccan Runes. Widdershins go by waning moon, chanting out thy baneful tune."* This lesson is perhaps the most complex of all the Wiccan Rede's teachings, for within it are contained the secrets of the directions and activities of celestial bodies, runology, and curses.[1] This chapter is broken into three sections to coherently examine these multifaceted teachings.

Concerning the Movements of Celestial Bodies

Pagans and witches have always looked to the heavens for wisdom and inspiration. Through observing nature and their surroundings, both terrestrial as well as celestial, they discovered the forces of the universe and learned how to work with them for the benefit of all.

In Wicca, one of the most important, if not *the* most important, of the heavenly bodies is the moon. For centuries, science has understood the vast influence that the moon has upon the Earth. For instance, the ebb and flow of our world's oceans is governed by the gravitational pull of the moon. It is safe to say that since the

---

[1] Considering the nature of the Threefold Law, as well as the Wiccan Rede itself, it would suffice to say that witches do not cast curses or hex their enemies. However, it is imperative to understand how these enchantments are employed, and why they work, for a well-balanced understanding of occult theory and mechanics.

moon's forces can be felt on a body of water as immense as all the Earth's oceans, then a subject as small as a human body, which incidentally is made up of mostly water, is just as likely to be influenced by those same lunar forces.

In nature, all things rotate in a deosil, or Sun-wise, pattern. The sun, moon, planets, and stars all rise in the east and set in the west. This Sun-wise motion of the heavenly bodies was observed by the ancient pagans as being the proper direction of all nature and was incorporated into their ancient religious and magickal rites. When casting a circle, it is proper for the circle to be cast deosil, or clockwise, to insure the circle's utmost strength. When stirring a cauldron the same holds true—stir deosil for constructive magick. Likewise widdershins, or a counter-clockwise motion, was considered improper and frowned upon because it went against the very direction of nature. Incidentally, many negative spells and curses call for the circle to be cast widdershins precisely for this reason—it violates natural law.

Not only is the path through the heavens that the moon follows important, but the actual rotations of the moon itself are equally important. When the moon rotates from the New to the Full, it is said that the moon waxes, and during this period of time it is believed by witches to be beneficial for constructive magic. Work spells of a positive nature during the period of the waxing moon (i.e., to get a better job, find a house or apartment, obtain money, etc.). When the moon rotates from the Full to the New, it is said that the moon wanes, and during this period of time it is believed by witches to be beneficial for destructive magick. Work spells of a negative nature during the period of the waning moon (i.e., to destroy an illness, curb a bad habit, stop a tornado, etc.).

Understanding the laws of nature and the overall scheme of the universe is an intricate part of practicing Wicca.

The Seax-Wiccan Runes

When the Wiccan Rede was first penned over twenty years ago, this couplet was written as "*Deosil go by waxing moon, chanting out the Wiccan Runes.*" The Theban system is usually referred to, although erroneously, as the Witch's runes. However, the Theban alphabet is actually an arcane system of writing that was created during the seventeenth century and is not an authentic runic system. Over the past two decades, significant discoveries have been made in both magick as well as archaeology, which have shed considerable light on runology. Raymond Buckland claims, on page sixteen of his book *The Tree: Complete Book of Saxon Witchcraft,* that the Seax-Wiccan Futhorc are in fact the original runes discovered by Odin when he hung on Yggdrasill.

Today, there are many runic systems in use by many different pagan traditions. The most commonly used system is the Elder Futhark, but through my research and findings, I have come to agree with Dr. Buckland pertaining to the belief of the superiority of the Seax-Wiccan Futhorc over all other runic systems. I have amended the sixth couplet of the Wiccan Rede for this reason.

Originally, runic inscriptions were carved in wood and leather but unfortunately, these have not survived to our present day. The few inscriptions that do survive were carved in metal and stone, and some of these have been proven to date as far back as 150 C.E. The blade of Ovre-Stabu, for example, found in Norway, is our oldest artifact to date, but the recent Meldorf archeological find may shed more quality evidence on when humanity began using the runes in an organized fashion. It has been speculated that since there is a lack of Saxon artifacts in recent archaeological discoveries, it is a major possibility that the Saxon Futhorc could be older than the Elder Futhark and other runic systems due to the perishable nature of the materials used for their inscriptions.

Each rune stave represents a single force in and of itself. Later, after experiences and observations were taken into account, the individual rune staves were organized into rows commonly referred to as Futhorc or Futhark (being named thusly after the first six rune staves in the row), and then later broken down even further into the *aett* categorization. It is curious to note that only the Elder Futhark and its later derivatives were broken down into these aett divisions.

Aett is the plural form of *aettrir*, which is an Old Norse term used to categorize items of similar attributes, usually in groups of eight. In this case, we see numerology playing an important roll in runic categorization, for the Elder Futhark is made up of twenty-four individual rune staves that are then broken down into three sets, or aett. Contrary to popular belief, the Seax-Wiccan Futhorc is not broken down into three sets of eight, but rather, because of its twenty-seven individual rune staves, it is divided into three groups of nine. It is because of this profound numerological difference that we can begin to understand the vastly supreme qualities of the Seax-Wiccan Futhorc.

Seax-Wica Futhorc

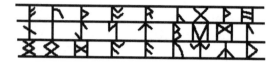

Various documentation concludes that the Saxon runes numbered anywhere from twenty-eight to thirty-three individual staves. My findings, based on data found in the *Elder Edda*, give the solid probability of there being only twenty-seven original rune staves. Verses 146 through 163 of the *Havamal* give the detailed account of the eighteen runic spells that Woden learned through his runic initiation on Yggdrasill. Mathematically, this equation can be reduced to a single number: $18 = 1 + 8 = 9$. Nine, being a significantly sacred number in ancient Teutonic philosophy, is then added to the original eighteen, thus creating the number twenty-seven. Interestingly, twenty-seven can then be reduced back to the number nine, showing the interdependent nature of this multi-faceted esoteric system. The entire equation looks like this: $18 = 1 + 8 = 9 + 18 = 27 = 2 + 7 = 9$.

According to ancient Teutonic lore, the number nine is extremely important and considered sacred. The number consistently reoccurs throughout the *Eddas* and *Sagas* of the Teutonic peoples. There are Nine Worlds in the system of Teutonic cosmology, and the human being is also made up of nine bodies, to name but a few examples, and so numerically we can see the importance that the number nine plays when studying runic lore.

Each rune of the Seax-Wiccan Futhorc is divided into three levels of power, which are set forth to further categorize the individual attributes of each rune. The three levels of power of each rune are as follows:

1. *Appearance:* the ideographic and phonic value of each rune
2. *Design:* the symbolic content of each rune's inherent nature
3. *Numerical:* the dynamic nature of each rune stave according to European numerology

Once again, we see numerology playing an important role in runic thought, and it is within the framework of this numerological importance that the superior qualities of the Seax-Wiccan Futhorc are discovered. As stated earlier, the Elder Futhark has twenty-four individual rune staves, which when divided are perfectly grouped in three sets of eight. Each rune stave is then further divided into a grouping of three attributes (i.e., appearance, design, and numerical). While the number twenty-four can be divided in three groups of eight, both the number eight and the number twenty-four are not advantageous to the formula needed for the successful completion of the equation culminating in runic superiority. Three, on the other hand, can go into nine and does so perfectly three times. With this information, we can begin to uncover the key to a major discovery, since three does in fact go into nine, not eight. Therefore the twenty-seven rune staves of the Seax-Wiccan Futhorc are more conducive for rune work, simply because the number twenty-seven can be divided by both three and nine, thus aligning the manifestation of the rune row with both the Teutonic cosmology as well as the *total* human being.

Further evidence of the numerical superiority of the Seax-Wiccan Futhorc is uncovered with the following numerological investigations. Let us first take the Elder Futhark, which contains twenty-four rune staves as previously mentioned. The number twenty-four can be reduced to its single numerical value with the formula $24 = 2 + 4 = 6$. While the number three does fit nicely into both twenty-four and six, neither twenty-four nor six are compatible with the important number nine. On the other hand, the Seax-Wiccan Futhorc, made up of its twenty-seven rune staves, can be reduced to its single numerical value of nine quite easily by using the exact same formula: $27 = 2 + 7 = 9$. Again, we clearly see, using these equations, that the Seax-Wiccan Futhorc corresponds perfectly to the numerical value of not only the Nine Worlds, but also the nine bodies of humanity. Since Wicca is a nature-oriented religion, blending the forces of nature (the nine worlds) and the forces of each individual witch (the nine bodies) with the forces of the runes themselves, it is easy to comprehend the extreme importance for using the Seax-Wiccan Futhorc over other runic systems.

We can cross-reference the above findings with one more test, which will determine the total numerical value for each rune row, be it Futhorc or Futhark. First, we must add all of the individual runic values together for each rune row, thus giving us the total numerical value for that entire runic system. Using this formula, we can see that the Elder Futhark's total numerical value is three hundred. The number three hundred can then be rendered into a single numerical value by using the same formula as stated above: $300 = 3 + 0 + 0 = 3$. Consequently, the Seax-Wiccan Futhorc's total numerical value is three hundred and seventy-eight, which when reduced to a single numerical value, once again returns to nine as we see in the following equation: $378 = 3 + 7 + 8 = 18 = 1 + 8 = 9$. Again, we see that the number nine prevails.

While the Elder Futhark's total rune stave numerical

value is six, its total numerical value is three. When three is added to six it becomes nine, and this of course indeed proves that the Elder Futhark does possess some worth as a magickal tool. But it also shows evidence that it is inherently lacking in its overall magickal potential, since it does not possess the entire numerical value of the Nine Worlds. On the contrary, the Seax-Wiccan Futhorc contains the complete numerical value in both rune stave as well as its total.

The Runes and Our Human Birthright

A major goal in life is to achieve a state of being free from misery, pain, sorrow, disease, and old age. One of the primary aims of Wicca, and spirituality in general, is to remove these afflictions. Many religions, especially the new monotheistic religions, reject and often condemn practices of spiritual exercises (whether physical or academic) aimed at gaining higher insights into the Ultimate Truths of existence. Such methods are feared by the established organized religions because of the spiritual independence experienced by their congregations when these afflictions are removed. To combat this possibility, they control their congregations through tactics of fear and guilt, and by forbidding the practice of these so-called New Age concepts and ideas.

We need not be held prisoner by these outdated medieval tactics though, for the use of the runes are our innate birthright, if we only have the courage to open ourselves up to their power. Before we go any further, let us now look at how deeply the runes permeate our very being. Indeed, we will come to discover that the energy of the runes is inherent in our very DNA!

When discussing runic lore, we can see that the energy of the runes themselves is caught up in the very process of material creation. The runes have no point of origin, for they are eternal and timeless; therefore it is to be understood that they are the essence of the energy located at the very heart of Ginnungagap.

When the Nine Worlds began to emerge from Ginnungagap, the runic forces were subjected to a high level of polarization. Dr. Thorsson, in his book *Futhark*, claims the runes were then divided equally, half becoming shining runes (*heidhrunar*) and the other half becoming dark runes (*myrkrunar*). While this hypothesis seems to work for the twenty-four runes of the Elder Futhark, we soon discover through numerical investigation that there is a major problem with this line of thought. While Dr. Thorsson is correct concerning the polarizing aspects of heidhrunar and myrkrunar, we must take into account the fact that the Seax-Wiccan Futhorc will behave differently from the Elder Futhark, even under the exact same cosmic conditions, thus showing evidence of their superiority as the *original* runic force.

Continuing with his essay in *Futhark*, Dr. Thorsson writes:

"These are polarized aspects of the entire corpus of runic power expressed simultaneously. These forces attract one another, in order that they might rejoin and create the cosmic seed manifestation contained in Ymir. The shining runes and dark runes are reassimilated in a pattern capable of manifestation. The runic forces are at work throughout the cosmogonic process described above; however, the runes as we know them have not been manifested, because the entire process, up to the sacrifice of Ymir, takes place in an unmanifested state. When Odhinn, Vili, and Ve sacrifice Ymir (the crystallized seed form of the collective runic pattern), they arrange this runic substance in accord with the multiversal pattern. Thus they create the Nine Worlds and Yggdrasill. This primal act brings about cosmic order and manifestation. At this point the runes are ordered in the Futhark row in their linear form as the primary arrangement at the center of the multiverse. This manifestation unfolds from the inside out, beginning with the most basic forms of cycli-

cal (*jera*) and vertical (*iwas*) force. From that point
the other runes manifest themselves in a linear
pattern governed by a twelve-fold spherical law.
As each succeeding circle is manifested, a pair of
runes—esoteric concepts—are isolated within
the space. The laws of sympathy and antipathy
determine which runes crystallize in each circle.
Also, those same laws govern which of these two
concepts will be aligned with which previously
manifested rune in the row. The row thus pro-
duced is perceived by the intellect in an order
governed by the path of the sun, and thereby the
runes manifest their numerical value one through
twenty-four. These numerical values are also part
of the innate relative positions of one mystery to
the others, and play a determining role in their
ordering. These patterns, as well as those that
govern the linear alignment of the staves, are
fruitful avenues of meditation and will reveal
much wisdom and provide great power to the
vitki who can unravel their riddles."

By using Dr. Thorsson's equation we begin to see dis-
crepancies when using the Elder Futhark. As stated earlier, the Elder Futhark does not properly function
numerically when working this, or any, numerical equation. At first things might seem to coincide with each

other quite nicely. The twenty-four runes divide perfectly into a twelve-fold spherical law, and this seems to explain the polarization aspect of the runes themselves. But upon closer inspection we discover two important things: (1) neither twenty-four nor twelve is reducible to the magickally important number of nine, and (2) change only takes place when a balance of force is upset. Since twelve goes into twenty-four perfectly, there is no innate upsetting of the balance within the rune row—therefore change is impossible. To further examine this problem we must take into serious consideration that since, due to this equation, change is impossible, the energy needed to cause the emergence of the Nine Worlds from Ginnungagap is not forthcoming.

Dr. Thorsson may indeed have had some insight on this problem when he later said, "This represents only one of several patterns in which the runes are arranged or divided—each world or realm of being has its own particular modality. The *aettir* are ruled by the pattern of the eightfold cross or star by which the ancient Northmen divided the heavens."

This being said, we should now look at other possibilities using this same equation, but with the Seax-Wiccan Futhorc instead, to see if other patterns do in fact reveal themselves.

As we have already discovered earlier, the twenty-seven staves of the Seax-Wiccan Futhorc reduce to nine perfectly, which gives us the starting point. Since twenty-seven does not reduce in any way to eight, we can see some conflict of balance begin to occur when the Seax-Wiccan Futhorc is arranged on the above-mentioned eight-fold cross.

By seeing how the rune staves are arranged, we see the upset of runic balance grow quite steadily. Another thing to take into consideration is the fact that the twenty-seven rune staves cannot be divided equally in half, and this, coupled with the fact that the Seax-Wiccan Futhorc does not even contain the cyclical rune *jera*, which was the matrix point in Dr. Thorsson's formula, we discover that it is essentially impossible for the rune row to correctly align itself to itself in the manner explained by Dr. Thorsson. On the other hand, when the polarizing aspects of the unmanifested runic energy begin to manifest, due to the change created by the increasing imbalance of runic force, minute similarities begin to repel themselves at the same instant that opposites begin attracting themselves. What then takes shape is a universally potent runic energy strand.

Upon closer investigation it is revealed to us that this runic anomaly is essentially the primordial material structure of the universal DNA double helix scattered randomly throughout the cosmos.

Knowing this, I believe it is safe to say that even though the Gods gave birth to humanity with Woden's gift of vital breath, it was initially the runes that gave birth to the Gods. Since we can, by means of the formula mentioned earlier, easily trace our life essence directly to Woden himself, and likewise, Woden's life essence can be traced back to the runic force that actually manifested material existence, we can then understand that tapping into this runic God-Force is not only possible, but is our inherited birthright. This being said, I would like to encourage all practitioners of Wiccan to eagerly and persistently dive deeper into these deep philosophical teachings, for we are just beginning to unlock the secrets contained in these ancient mysteries.

It is common knowledge that the runes are hidden in mystery, and yet the mysteries hidden within the runes themselves are immeasurable. The early Runemasters taught this esoteric wisdom only to the initiated apprentice, and even then, the knowledge was slow in coming. Today this knowledge is no longer hidden, but exoteric, and available to the uninitiated public. This is as it should be, for the use of the runes is our birthright. We have discovered through our simple, yet thorough, investigations that even though the runes are eternal, without beginning or end, Odin's self-sacrifice brought forth the manifestation of the rune row for the benefit of humanity. We can also see how volatile this rune row is, and how it has changed over the centuries, in accordance with the essential needs of humanity. Indeed, within each rune is a universe of change, and thus need for change is what brought the Nine Worlds out from the depths of Ginnungagap. It is also this need for change that will annihilate the Nine Worlds at Ragnarok. Today we continue to grasp for truths, for truth does not change with age. The only question now left unanswered is *Can we handle the consequences of that Truth, and wield the wisdom responsibly?* If one lives by the code that is the Wiccan Rede, then the answer to this question is a definite yes!

Basics of Negative Magick

In the physical world, opposites attract. In the spiritual world, similarities attract. This principle of *sympathy* is the underlying secret of all magick. In many magickal systems, such as voodoo, Santeria, and witchcraft, the practice of sympathetic magic is not alien. Vivid images of African witch doctors and Haitian witches jabbing pins in dolls to curse one's enemies are laced through many an ancient tale. The mechanics behind such activities are simple. The witch visualizes the doll as being the actual person, the very target and receptacle for intense negative energy. Whatever happens to the doll will happen to the person that the doll represents. This practice can even be found in various papyrus scrolls of the XVIII Dynasty of Egypt, verifying conclusively its dark and ancient roots.

Accompanying the physical and celestial preparations of these baneful spells are their vocal incantations. These human-created vibrations of sound tie the terrestrial aspects of the curse to the celestial for added power. Knowing this, one can see the very simple formula for negative magick: *Proper timing (waning phase of the moon, as shown earlier), working in a widdershins direction (casting the circle, stirring a cauldron, dancing, walking, etc.), combined with the use of sympathy (making an effigy in the image of the enemy), and baneful incantation.* Of course, there are other aspects of negative magick that can be employed for effective cursing and hexing, such as colors (e.g., black) and herbs (e.g., poisonous).

Even though witches should not get into the habit of casting curses or hexes, or practicing negative magick, we should learn the basic details of such workings. Understanding the heavy weight that the Three-Fold Law carries will make us think twice about harming another, through magick or otherwise, although we do have the right to protect ourselves. We also have the option of petitioning our Gods for justice when we have been wronged by another! However, before such a petition is made, one should do quite a bit of soul searching, for justice may be extracted not only against your enemy, but might be executed against you as well. Every physical being is fallible and imperfect—our enemies as well as ourselves. This important fact must always be kept in mind before working any magick, negative or otherwise.

Fully comprehending the basics of baneful magick will give one a better grasp of defensive magick. Below is an example of a *justice*-type curse. This spell is given as an example of the theory of baneful magick, and its employment and execution is not condoned by the author or the publisher.

Basic Curse of Justice

This magickal working is best performed during the period of the waning moon. Assemble the following items and arrange them on your altar: a black cloth bag, two black candles, an effigy of your intended target, nine rusty pins, and an iron cauldron.

Position your altar to face either north or east. Start a fire in the iron cauldron and place it on the ground, south of your altar. Set the two black candles on the left and right side of your altar. Place the effigy of your enemy between the candles. Spend a few minutes in silent meditation contemplating the wrongs that have been committed against you, as well as the task at hand. At this time, it may be a good idea to recite the Wiccan Rede. If any adverse emotions arise before, during, or after the recital, rethink your decision to curse your enemy and terminate the working. If everything feels right, and you sincerely believe that justice needs to be extracted, continue with the ritual.[2]

Begin the ritual by lighting the two black candles and reciting the following words: *"The fire of justice is now heaped upon thee, [name of enemy], thou enemy of the Lord and Lady! The flame of justice prevails over your accursed soul and shade, and the flame of damnation shall gnaw into you!"*

While meditating on the injustices that have been heaped upon you by this enemy, take the nine rusty pins and begin jabbing them into the effigy while saying: *"Taste thou death, [name of enemy], get thee back and retreat, oh enemy of the Lord and Lady; fall down, be repulsed, get back and retreat! I have driven thee back, and I have cut thee into thousands of pieces! The great God triumphs over thee,*

---

[2]Prior to working any baneful magick, it is advised that you read Chapter Sixteen of this manual very carefully and thoroughly!

[name of enemy]! The great Goddess triumphs over thee, [name of enemy]! Taste thou death! Back fiend, an end to thee! Therefore, have I driven thee to be destroyed and therefore have I adjudged thee evil, an end to thee! Taste thou death! Thou shalt never rise again! I smite thee down upon thy face, [name of enemy], oh enemy of the Lord and Lady! The flame of justice, which is powerful against the Lord and Lady's enemies, hath cast thee down and advanceth against thee and now thou art thrust down into the flame! The great flame of justice triumpheth over thee; the great flame of justice it prevaileth over thee, the great flame of justice devoureth thee, and what escapeth from the fire hath no being! Get thee back, for thou art cut asunder, thy soul is shriveled up, thy accursed name, [name of enemy], is buried in oblivion, and silence is you."

Throw the effigy into the blazing flames of the iron cauldron. Allow the candles and the cauldron fire to extinguish itself. The curse is completed by gathering up the cauldron's ashes, as well as the melted black candle wax, in the black cloth bag and burying it in a remote graveyard the following day.

᠅

Required Reading for This Chapter

Agrippa, Henry Cornelius. *Three Books of Occult Philosophy*. Chthonios Books, 1986.

Barrett, Francis. *The Magus, or Celestial Intelligencer, Being a Complete System of Occult Philosophy*. Hyde Park University Books, 1967.

Farrar, Stewart and Janet. *The Witches' Way: Principles, Rituals, and Beliefs of Modern Witchcraft*. Robert Hale, 1984.

Terry, Patricia, and Charles W. Dunn. *Poems of the Vikings: The Elder Edda*. Merrill, 1969.

Valiente, Doreen. *Natural Magic*. St. Martin's, 1975.

Ventimiglia, Mark. *Wiccan Yoga*. Citadel Press, 2001.

7

OF LUNAR ASPECTS OF
MAGICK AND THE BASICS
OF OCCULT NUMEROLOGY

THE EIGHTH COUPLET of the Wiccan Rede teaches: *"When the Lady's moon is new, kiss the hand to her times two."* Although this lesson speaks of the moon and our Goddess' lunar aspect, we should interpret this teaching as a metaphor, since instructions considering lunar science was covered in the sixth and seventh couplets. Actually, the last line of the couplet, *"kiss the hand to her times two,"* gives us the clue into this lesson's real meaning: *The basics of occult numerology.*

The science of numbers has long been considered important. As far back as ancient Greece and Egypt, we can see the interest placed in numbers from the occultists and thinkers of the day; even philosophers such as Aristotle, Plato, and Socrates, put a high priority on the use of numbers where metaphysics were concerned.

By using the following numerical chart, one can convert words into numbers, thus giving people, places, and things a numerical value.

1	2	3	4	5	6	7	8	9
a	b	c	d	e	f	g	h	i
j	k	l	m	n	o	p	q	r
s	t	u	v	w	x	y	z	

By simply assigning each letter a corresponding number, and then adding the numbers together, one arrives at the *total numerical value* for the word being converted. Once the total numerical value is discovered, it is important to then reduce the number to its single value. Every compound number can be reduced to a prime number through the process of simple multiplication. Please see the following example for the conversion of the name John Doe.

$$1 + 6 + 8 + 5 + 4 + 6 + 5 = 35 = 3 + 5 = 8$$

J   o   h   n   D   o   e

In regards to people, there are two aspects to remember concerning a person's *Life Number: Their name and their birth date.* The Life Number of a person is as important as their zodiac sign, and in many cases is even more accurate in defining an individual's personality attributes and their overall mental and emotional idiosyncrasies. Numerological horoscopes are surprisingly accurate.

The Life Number of an individual is discovered primarily by their birth date. For example, if John Doe were born on March 7th, 1967, you would calculate his Life Number as follows:

March 7 1967
3 + 7 + 1 + 9 + 6 + 7 = 33 = 3 + 3 = 6

Since the date when a person was born is unalterable, this number is considered their *Primary Life Number*. The numerical value of an individual's name is important, but because names can be changed, this number is considered the *Secondary Life Number*, due to its impermanent nature. A person is said to possess great occult strengths if their *Primary Life Number* and their *Secondary Life Number* are the same. In some instances, where the two numbers are different, one can add both numbers together and then reduce the sum to a single digit to obtain a *Personal Power Number*. While this can be considered acceptable, the *Primary Life Number* still remains the most important number when casting horoscopes and defining personal traits.

Following is a brief, universally accepted description of each of the single primary numbers. Simply match the definition of the number to your *Primary Life Number*, *Secondary Life Number,* and *Personal Power Number* to cast numerological horoscopes.

1

Individuals whose Life Number is One are endowed with the pioneer spirit. They are explorers and innovators; these individuals possess powerful stamina, are capable of great achievements, and are born leaders.

> *Positive traits for these individuals:* independent, determined, creative, innovative, and original.
>
> *Negative traits for these individuals:* overbearing, jealous, selfish, and stubborn.
>
> *Best career choices:* creative work of all kinds, inventor, designer, engineer, or explorer.

In a personal relationship, you are compatible with numbers 1, **2**,[1] 3, 6, and **9**.

In a business relationship, you are compatible with numbers 1, **2**, 4, 5, 6, 8, and **9**.

---

[1] Bold numbers are best numerical matches.

2

Individuals whose Life Number is Two are gentle by nature. These people are artistic, imaginative, and romantic; usually more mental than physical.

Positive traits for these individuals: understanding, gentle, and well balanced.

Negative traits for these individuals: lack of self-confidence, self-conscious, and occasionally deceitful.

Best career choices: salesperson, clerk, agent, politician, diplomat, or teacher.

In a personal relationship, you are compatible with numbers 1, 2, 3, 4, 6, 7, 8, and 9.

In a business relationship, you are compatible with numbers 1, 4, 8, and 9.

3

Individuals whose Life Number is Three are endowed with a strong desire to rise in the world, and have the intestinal fortitude to actually achieve their goals. These people are usually original, observant, and willing to work hard. They are versatile, clever, and often very lucky.

> *Positive traits for these individuals:* witty, energetic, brilliant, and sociable.
>
> *Negative traits for these individuals:* easily bored and occasionally wasteful.
>
> *Best career choices:* journalist, writer, artist, musician, or entertainer.

In a personal relationship, you are compatible with numbers 1, 2, **6**, 7, and **9**.

In a business relationship, you are compatible with numbers 5, 6, 7, and **8**.

4

Individuals whose Life Number is Four are very organized, usually efficient, and extremely practical. These people manage finances well and are among the most sociable of individuals.

> *Positive traits for these individuals:* calm, practical, respectable, efficient, and faithful.
>
> *Negative traits for these individuals:* gloomy, careless, and stubborn.
>
> *Best career choices:* farmer, accountant, builder, artist, executive, engineer, and chemist.

In a personal relationship, you are compatible with numbers 2, 4, 6, **7**, 8, and 9.

In a business relationship, you are compatible with numbers 1, 2, **4**, 6, **7**, and **8**.

5

Individuals whose Life Number is Five embody the adventurous spirit and will try anything new and exciting. These people are highly talented, creative, clever, and original.

> *Positive traits for these individuals:* clever, resourceful, affectionate, and loyal.
>
> *Negative traits for these individuals:* lustful, unstable, nervous, and restless.
>
> *Best career choices:* communications, literary work of any kind, linguist, all things connected with the travel industry, and dealing with the public.

In a personal relationship, you are compatible with numbers 6, **8**, and 9.

In a business relationship, you are compatible with numbers 1, 3, **8**, and 9.

6

Individuals whose Life Number is Six are often romantically inclined, imaginative, and creative, with a touch of artistic expression. These people are peace loving, open minded, and well balanced.

> *Positive traits for these individuals:* reliable, loyal, creative, honest, and faithful.
> *Negative traits for these individuals:* selfish, arrogant, and fussy.
> *Best career choices:* nursing, medicine, veterinary, religious ministry, or marriage counseling.

In a personal relationship, you are compatible with numbers 1, 2, 3, 4, 5, **6**, **8**, and **9**.

In a business relationship, you are compatible with numbers 1, 3, 4, 8, and **9**.

7

Individuals whose Life Number is Seven are usually highly interested in mysticism and the occult. These people are intuitive and imaginative and need to achieve a good deal of personal success and recognition in order to feel fulfilled.

> *Positive traits for these individuals:* intellectual, passionate, understanding, and good natured.
> *Negative traits for these individuals:* occasionally lazy, dreamy, moody, impractical, and depressive.

Best career choices: research or library work of an occult or metaphysical nature, archaeologist, astrologer, or philosopher.

In a personal relationship, you are compatible with numbers 2, 3, **4**, **7**, 8, and **9**.

In a business relationship, you are compatible with numbers 3, **4**, and **8**.

8

Individuals whose Life Number is Eight are endowed with an ambitious nature and prone to be highly energetic.

Positive traits for these individuals: ambitious, self-control, sound judgment, and energetic.

Negative traits for these individuals: arrogant, self-centered, and overly aggressive.

Best career choices: business executive, banker, stockbroker, lawyer, supervisor of any kind, or a business consultant and organizer.

In a personal relationship, you are compatible with numbers 2, 4, **5**, **6**, 7, and 9.

In a business relationship, you are compatible with numbers 1, 2, **3**, **4**, 6, **7**, and 9.

9

Individuals whose Life Number is Nine possess courage with a hint of selflessness. These people are generally concerned with humanity. They are often gifted artistically, possess a vast imagination, and are quick thinkers.

> *Positive traits for these individuals:* successful, spiritual, inspiring, and ambitious.
>
> *Negative traits for these individuals:* deceptive and occasionally impulsive.
>
> *Best career choices:* teacher, doctor, soldier, diplomat, and politician.

In a personal relationship, you are compatible with numbers **1**, **2**, **3**, 4, 5, **6**, **7**, 8, and **9**.

In a business relationship, you are compatible with numbers **1**, **2**, 5, **6**, and 9.

☙

Required Reading for This Chapter

Lane, Julia. *The Numerology Workbook*. Sterling, 1985.

☙

8

The Need to Love

THE NINTH COUPLET of the Wiccan Rede teaches: "*When the moon rides at her peak, then thou heart's desire seek.*" Even though we learned the basics of lunar timing and moon magic in the seventh chapter of this book, when we study the Wiccan Rede in detail we begin to comprehend the vast importance that the moon plays in Wiccan philosophy and its belief system. Out of the twenty-six couplets of this epic poem, four are devoted to the instruction of lunar magick and our Goddess' celestial attributes.

Reflecting back on the details of lunar timing, we remember that the moon has two cycles. When the moon is waxing, it is the most appropriate time to work constructive magic. When the moon is waning, it is the most appropriate time to work destructive magic. The moon is at its peak when it is full. The night of the full moon is the last day of the moon's waxing cycle, and therefore the most appropriate day for working constructive magic.

The second line of this couplet, "*then thou heart's desire seek*," explains true human nature: *The need to love, and be loved*. There are many reasons for casting positive spells—to obtain money, to secure protection, to increase health and longevity—yet of all the magic spells employed, I think it is safe to say that love spells are cast more than any other. And why is that? Human beings are social animals. We thrive in groups and communities, and wane in isolation. Knowing this, we can understand the extreme importance of love. Each of us needs to feel needed, appreciated, and loved. The Old Norse saying "*The pine withers in an open field with neither bark nor needles for protection. So too withers the person whom no one loves*,"[1] explains this idea perfectly.

One aspect of our Eternal Mother is that of a love deity. This can be seen in many of the world's myths and legends concerning the Goddess' lunar attributes. Tales detailing the activities of Aphrodite, Venus, Isis, Freya, and many others show how our Eternal Mother, in her many guises, weaves her love magick for the benefit of the entire world. Love is the strongest emotion, and truly, the most powerful form of magick.

One thing we should always keep in the forefront of our minds when working love magick is the fact that

[1] *Havamal*, verse 50.

we should never be manipulative in our spells. To cast an enchantment over a specific person to make that person fall in love with you violates the Wiccan Rede. One should never set out to control another.

So then, how does one work love magick in a non-manipulative, constructive way? That questing is easily answered by common sense: *Cast the spell on yourself to make yourself more attractive to the opposite sex.*[2] In this manner, you allow the magick to work on you, drawing a compatible mate to yourself, without interfering with the free will of another. An example of this can be seen in the two following prayers.

Prayer to Find a Compatible Spouse[3]

Dearest Mother,[4] I want to marry, but I have not met the right person. Please lead me to someone who will

---

[2] Since Wicca is a nature-based religion, it is every Wiccan's duty to observe the workings of nature to obtain a complete and unbiased understanding of our universe. Since many say the duality of nature is supported by the universal male-female union (ie: *the Lord and the Lady*), some feel that homosexuality is an affront to the God and Goddess, although many others disagree. In my personal opinion, Wiccans are not hedonists; we must not get caught up in stereotypes and fall prey to the old cliché "*Do what feels good.*" What feels good is not always what is right, moral, or ethical.

[3] Ventimiglia, Mark. *The Wiccan Prayer Book.* New York: Citadel Press, 2000, page 130.

[4] Women can pray to the God, and men to the Goddess, if so desired.

love me and understand me, and whom I can love and understand; someone with whom I can share the joys of a Wiccan life.

Thank you, Mother, for I have faith that you have heard me and will answer my prayer. Blessed be.

Prayer for Friendship[5]

Dear Father, I know that I am never truly alone in this world. I know that you are always near me. But, Lord, even knowing this, I sometimes feel great despair and loneliness. Please send me a special friend, someone I can trust and confide in.

Dear Mother, loving friend, please give me the gift of friendship, so that I will never be alone. Give me the strength to see the light of the God and Goddess in everyone I meet. So mote it be.

Some Basics of Love Magick

Love magic, like any other type of spellwork, can be as simple or as complex as the witch desires. One can either cast a quick enchantment or perform a full-blown magickal ritual. The choice is yours.

---

[5] Ventimiglia, Mark. *The Wiccan Prayer Book*. New York: Citadel Press, 2000, page 127.

For simple enchantments, there are four key elements[6] needed for a successful working. These are: lunar timing, the proper herbs, an appropriate color, and of course, the incantation itself. More complex spells can employ the use of incense, oils, potions, astrology, numerology, and many other occult and metaphysical tools. Below is a brief list of some basic love spells. From this list, you will be able to obtain a good degree of knowledge about crafting your own enchantments and designing your own spells. Access the glossary for definitions of unfamiliar words and phrases.

Basic Love Spell #1

On the night of the full moon, take one red candle and inscribe the word *LOVE* in its wax with your athame. Light the candle and recite the following phrase three times: *"By the aid of Aphrodite, bring love to me!"* Allow the candle to extinguish itself. The spell is done.

Basic Love Spell #2

Gather fresh red roses on the night of the new moon. Remove the rose petals from the stems and allow to

---

[6]The witch can use any combination of these four elements in any given working.

dry for the following two weeks. On the night of the full moon, take the dried rose petals and cast them onto a lit charcoal. As the sweet fragrance of the rose is released as incense, recite the following incantation: *"May this incense carry my plea to heaven's gate, and grant me my wish for a compatible mate."*

Basic Love Spell #3

Obtain a good degree of fresh rosemary, rose petals, basil, and one ripe avocado. Add all ingredients to a blender and puree into a thick paste. Pour the mixture into an airtight container and refrigerate. On the night of the full moon, take the mixture and spread it on your face as a mud mask, while visualizing yourself becoming more beautiful and desirable to the opposite sex. The following morning, simply wash your face clean and know that the spell is complete.

Basic Love Spell #4

To make a love charm, simply sew nine apple seeds into a small red cloth band and wear to attract love.

Basic Love Spell #5

Obtain a short piece of red yarn and craft it into a bracelet or anklet. On the night of the new moon, put on the bracelet or anklet and do not remove it until the day of the full moon. On the night of the full moon, go outside and petition the Goddess in your own words to bring you true love, and then bury the yarn in your yard to complete the spell. If you live in an apartment complex and do not have a yard, simply take the yarn to a secluded spot like a wood or a park and bury it there.

Basic Love Spell #6

For those witches who live by the sea, you can obtain the eternal energy of the ocean to aid your spell. The constant caresses of the ocean waves on the seashore greatly complements love magick.

At low tide,[7] on the night of the full moon, walk barefoot along the seashore visualizing your true love. With a long branch of Elm, inscribe the words *BRING TRUE LOVE TO ME* in the sand near the water's edge. Walk away without looking back, knowing that the Goddess will answer your request.

---

[7]It is important to do this spell at low tide, because once the tide rises, it will overtake your inscription and absorb your intention with the eternal energies of the sea, thus guaranteeing success.

Basic Love Spell #7

Fill your bathtub with lukewarm water. To this, add a pinch of ground rosemary, catnip, chamomile, cinnamon, and lemon juice. Light nine red candles and place them around your bathtub. Turn off all lights in the bathroom and open the window to allow the entire room to be bathed in the light of the full moon. Soak in this moon bath for as long as you feel necessary. Allow the candles to burn themselves out to complete the spell.

Basic Love Spell #8

On the eve of the full moon, go to a secluded location. For a few moments, gaze at the beauty of the moon while visualizing your need to find true love, or obtain a mate. Make a prayer request to the Goddess. You can use one of the two prayers listed in this chapter or you can construct your own. Using your power (dominant) hand, toss a handful of hazelnuts up into the air. It is done.

Basic Love Spell #9

Wear a dab of rose oil behind each ear to attract true love.

Basic Love Spell #10

Carrying a sprig of dried mistletoe will attract love.

Required Reading for This Chapter

Monaghan, Patricia. *The New Book of Goddesses and Heroines*. E. P. Dutton, 1981.

Morrison, Sarah L. *The Modern Witch's Spellbook*. Citadel Press, 1973.

9

THE FOUR DIRECTIONS

COUPLETS TEN THROUGH THIRTEEN of the Wiccan Rede teach: "*Heed the north wind's mighty gale, lock the door an' trim the sail. When the wind comes from the south, love will kiss thee on the mouth. When the wind blows from the west, departed spirits have no rest. When the wind blows from the east, expect the new an' set the feast.*" This lesson strictly concerns itself with the elemental magick of the four winds.

Many pagan cultures considered the winds to be spirits, divine beings, or deities. Nowhere was this more true than in the Greek and Roman states. In Homer, for example, the four chief winds are mentioned.[1] In Athens, Greece,[2] stands the *Tower of the Winds*, where the names of the eight winds are preserved in stone.[3]

---

[1] *Boreas* (north), *Zephyrus* (west), *Eurus* (east) and *Notus* (south).

[2] Seyffert, Oskar. *The Dictionary of Classical Mythology, Religion, Literature, and Art.* Portland House Publishing, 1995.

[3] *Boreas* (north), *Kaikias* (northeast), *Apeliotes* (east) *Eurus* (southeast), *Notus* (south), *Lips* (southwest), *Zephyrus* (west), and *Argestes* (northwest).

According to one mythological account, the God Zeus appointed Aeolus as the caretaker of the winds. However, in other tales, the winds are seen as independent beings, that obey the commands of Zeus and the other Gods. The winds were also occasionally invoked by men through means of prayers and sacrifices.[4]

The Greek poet Hesiod[5] calls the beneficent winds the *Children of Astraeus and Eos*, and makes the distinction between them and the destructive winds, calling the latter the *Children of Typhoeus*.[6] Other legends speak only of Boreas and Zephyrus, from whose loins sprang the many lines of mythical steeds. The Harpyiae were the swift-footed Goddesses of the sweeping storm, yet Homer named only one of these deities: *Podarge*. From the union of Zephyrus and Podarge came the famous horses of Achilles.

There are many purposes for invoking the spirits of the winds and utilizing their beneficial attributes in one's magickal workings. For instance, a sailor can summon a breeze to fill a sail, or a farmer can invoke the winds to blow in rain clouds to water a field. We can even weave protection spells to appease the wind spirits, thus guarding ourselves from malevolent weather.

[4]Blood sacrifices are not, and never were, a practice of Wicca.

[5]Hesiod was a Greek poet who lived after Homer, most likely around 776 B.C.E.

[6]We get the word *typhoon* from the Greek *Typhoeus*.

It should be remembered that when invoking a particular wind, the wind invoked is the one that blows *from* that particular direction rather than *to* that direction. For example, the north wind blows *from* the north; therefore, a north wind will generate a southern breeze. When weaving enchantments concerning the winds, please keep this important directional detail in mind.

Basic Wind Magick

To Invoke the North Wind

During hot days when a cool breeze is needed, invoke the north wind by chanting: "*Oh mighty Boreas, who hails from the frozen north, blow your gentle arctic winds across tundra and frozen sea; reduce the heat and refresh me!*"

To Invoke the South Wind

In the midst of winter, when the air is frigid and the temperature drops to subzero, a simple invocation of the south wind can bring immediate relief. The invocation to the south wind is thus: "*Notus, Notus, Notus, oh mighty wind of the fiery south, remove the chill and warm my house!*"

To Invoke the East Wind

To cause a breeze to blow from the east, chant the following incantation: "*Eurus the mighty, Eurus the strong, bring me an east wind that will blow all day long!*"

To Invoke the West Wind

To summon a west wind, chant the following incantation: "*Zephyrus Sasnakra Thar Thar Thamaru Mommon Betos Opranu!*"

Protection from Storms

If there is foul weather in the forecast that calls for dangerous storms and high winds, you can protect your home by simply sprinkling salt around the perimeter of your property. Drawing a circle of salt around the exterior of your home will guard it from storms and adverse weather.

Protection from Tornados

Obtain four knives. Their condition is not important, but they must be sharp. Bury one knife, blade tip pointing skyward, on each side of the house. No matter which way the twister comes from, it will be *cut in twain* by the sharp blade of the buried knife, thus protecting your home.

The Weathervane or Windsock

Concerning these four couplets directly, one should either purchase a weathervane or build a windsock in order to monitor random wind occurrences. These random occurrences pertain to the activities of the winds that you have *not* invoked, and they relate directly to ancient pagan lore.

For instance, the tenth couplet, "*Heed the north wind's mighty gale, lock the door an' trim the sail,*" warns of storms and destructive winds. If you gaze upon your weathervane or windsock and it shows that a north wind is beginning to stir, you would be best advised to secure your home against a coming storm. When your weathervane or windsock indicates a southerly wind, be ready to meet a new love interest, as the eleventh couplet informs, "*When the wind comes from the south, love will kiss thee on the mouth.*" An uninvoked westerly wind has the ability to wrestle spirits from their graves, therefore if you live near a cemetery, a western breeze may cause the spirits to stir and therefore cause mischief in or near your home. And lastly, the thirteenth couplet of the Wiccan Rede tells us that when our wind device shows an easterly wind blowing, one had better set a few more places at the dinner table, since unexpected company is on the way!

Required Reading for This Chapter

Cunningham, Scott. *Earth Power*. Llewellyn, 1983.

Sharon, Douglas. *Wizard of the Four Winds: A Shaman's Story*. Free Press, 1978.

Weinstein, Marion. *Earth Magic: A Dianic Book of Shadows*. Earth Magic Productions, 1980.

10

HERBALISM

THE FOURTEENTH AND FIFTEENTH COUPLET of the Wiccan Rede teaches: *"Nine woods in the cauldron go, burn them fast an' burn them slow. Elder be the Lady's tree, burn it not or cursed thou'll be,"* which is a basic lesson for pagan herbology, and directly relates to the eighteenth couplet: *"Heed ye flower, bush an' tree, by the Lady, blessed be."*

While the subject of herbology is vast, and an in-depth book on the matter would take up the space double or even triple the size of this book, I will just make references to the herbs directly pertaining to these three couplets. You are encouraged to do further studying on the subject of herbology on your own, and the few books listed in the required reading list at the end of this chapter are good places for you to start.

According to the Wiccan Rede, there are nine herbs common to the use of Wicca. These herbs are used for magick, as well as for medicine. A precautionary note must always be kept in mind concerning the medicinal uses of herbs, especially when taken internally: Even though herbs are natural substances and are usually not as harsh as man-made synthetic drugs, one should still exercise a degree of caution and respect when using them. The old saying holds true even today: *"Herbs that can heal can also harm."*

The Nine Herbs

Catnip (*nepeta cataria*): Catnip is a wonderful herb and is sacred to the Egyptian cat Goddess, Bast. Knowing this, you can sew some up in a small sachet and give it to your favorite feline as an intoxicating gift. It will strengthen the physical as well as psychic bonds of your relationship.

Catnip, when used with roses, makes a nice sachet for successful love charms. You can also hang a sprig or two of catnip over the front door of your home to attract friends, good luck, and beneficial spirit entities. For medicinal purposes, brew a small bit of the herb as a warm tea before retiring for the night and you will have a comforting sleep and prophetic dreams.

Coltsfoot (*tussilago farfara*): Coltsfoot is an incredibly useful herb. There are many international folk names for the plant, such as *British Tobacco, Bull's Foot, Pas d' ana* (French), and *Sponnc* (Irish), which is evidence of its widespread use. It is considered as being of female gender, and is sacred to the love deity, Venus.

Coltsfoot can be sewn in sachets as a love charm, or brewed in a tea as a love philter. When brewed in a tea with chamomile, and drunk by lovers in the evening, it makes for a relaxing aphrodisiac.

If the dried leaves of coltsfoot are smoked, prophetic visions are granted by the Gods.

Comfrey (*symphytum officinale*): The two most common uses for the herb comfrey are protection during one's travels and granting a much-needed increase in money.

If you are planning a trip abroad, simply pack a sprig or two in your luggage and carry a bit of the ground herb on your person, preferably in a small sachet.

To increase your wealth, simply burn a small amount of comfrey in your cauldron over lit charcoal while chanting the following incantation: "*Dearest God, Dearest Goddess, hear me now as I burn this comfrey, bring me wealth, bring me money!*"

Garlic (*allium sativum*): Probably the oldest herb ever used in pagan rites and folk magick is garlic. Even today, we remember the old folk belief that garlic protects against vampires and werewolves. During the dark ages in Europe, the herb was also used as a charm for protection against the deadly bubonic plague. Today garlic is used not only as a wonderful culinary spice, but also in medicine. Medical science has recognized the herb's wonderful healing properties and recommends taking at least 300 milligrams a day to remain in optimal health.

Magickally, garlic is sacred to the dark Goddess Hecate, and thus is used in rites of protection and exorcism. Since garlic has destructive properties, the herb is also used in healing spells where the destruction of an illness is needed.

Ginger (*zingiber officinalis*): Ginger is useful for attracting love, money, success, and power. This herb can be used externally, in magick, or taken internally, in a tea or as a ground spice.

Prior to working any magick or performing any ritual, drink ginger tea or sprinkle the ground herb onto your food. This will increase your magickal energies and bring added success to your ritual or spellwork.

Lobelia (*lobelia inflata*): Lobelia has unfairly received a bad reputation, for the herb is a powerful medicinal purgative and every pagan household should keep some in the herb cabinet for emergencies. The many medicinal attributes can be seen in the old folk names of the herb: *asthma weed, bladderpod, gagroot, and pukeweed*. Since lobelia is extremely powerful, one should experiment carefully when using the herb internally.

Ancient lore calls for growing lobelia in the garden, thus protecting one's home and property from storms, as well as for attracting love and tranquility to the household.

Plaintain (*plantago*): Plaintain is a wonderful and useful herb, and grows wild all through the continental United States. Magickally, the herb can be used for protection, healing, and gaining strength. Old folklore claims that plaintain guards the bearer from poisonous snakebites.

Taken internally, plaintain is a high source of calcium and Vitamin A. Toss the fresh leaves in a salad or steep in a warm tea.

Valerian (*valeriana officinalis*): Valerian is another herb that is sacred to Venus, the love Goddess. Knowing this, the herb can be used in love magick as well as an aphrodisiac. Valerian's other magickal attributes include a cure for insomnia, purification, and protection.

Vervain (*verbena officinalis*): Probably one of the strongest of the nine magickal herbs is vervain. This herb is sacred to the deities Juno, Thor, Jupiter, Isis, Mars, Venus, Aradia, and Kerridwen. Its magickal properties include attracting love, gaining protection and purification, obtaining peace and tranquility, as well as acquiring money and wealth. Vervain is also a wonderful sleep aid. It can be used for healing the body and the mind, and grants youthfulness.

Elder *(sambucus canadensis)*: The fifteenth couplet of the Wiccan Rede is a warning as well as a lesson: *"Elder be the Lady's tree, burn it not or cursed thou'll be."* Elder is called the Lady's tree because it is sacred to the deities Venus and Holda, and has long been venerated in witchcraft and Wicca. While it is acceptable to use the wood and leaves of this tree in rites and spells, it should never be burned! Exorcism, healing, and gaining prosperity are among its magickal attributes. Use elder with respect!

The eighteenth couplet and the final lesson of this chapter reads: *"Heed ye flower, bush an' tree."* This phrase directly relates to the old pagan magical trio of the *Oak* (*quercus alba*), *Ash* (*fraxinus excelsior*), and *Thorn* (*crataegus oxacantha*). However, the phrasing in the poem is slightly incorrect, since the Oak and the Ash are both trees, while the Hawthorn is both a bush and a thorn. Interesting to note, no flower was ever named in the old pagan saying, even though the Hawthorn does in fact flower. Below are the attributes of these three powerful magickal plants.

Oak *(quercus alba)*: The mighty Oak has long been used in magick by witches and druids alike. It is sacred to the deities Dagda, Jupiter, Thor, Zeus, Herne, Pan, and Hecate. Use Oak in spells and enchantments for gaining protection, health, money, and fertility. One can increase luck by simply carrying acorns. The bark, wood, leaves, and nuts of this tree can all be used in magick and ritual.

Ash (*fraxinus excelsior*): In ancient Teutonic lore, it is said that the mighty World Tree, *Yggdrasill*, is a giant Ash; from this tree, the God Odin hung for nine days and nine nights and was granted the discovery of the runic mysteries. The Ash is sacred to Odin, Thor, Gwydion, Mars, Neptune, Poseidon, and Uranus. Its wood, bark, and leaves can be used for protection during sea voyages, for gaining wealth, and for maintaining one's health. A wand or staff of Ash is considered a very powerful magickal tool.

Hawthorn (*crataegus oxacantha*): The use of Hawthorn extends as far back into history as ancient Roman times. Romans used to place a few Hawthorn leaves in the cradles of babies to guard the infants from evil spirits. Today, the herb can still be used in magick as a powerful protective aid, as well as taken internally to grant strength to a weak heart.

It is said that Hawthorn is sacred to the fairies and when grown in a grove with Oaks and Ashes, it grants the ability to see the Little People, if one visits the grove on the night of a full moon.

Basics of Herbal Measurements

When working with herbs, especially for their medicinal properties, it is extremely important to respect their attributes. Even though many herbs are non-toxic and contain vast healing powers, too much of any one thing is never good. One piece of advice: *Handle with care!* The following conversion table will help you in measuring out specific dosages.

As mentioned earlier, the science of herbology is vast. Intelligent Wiccans are well advised to diligently pursue the study of herbal lore and familiarize themselves with as much of the subject as possible. The few individual herbs listed in this chapter are a good place to begin, but understand that this short list merely scratches the surface of this infinite and fascinating subject.

CONVERSION TABLE

1/8 fl.oz	= 1 dram	= 1/2 tsp + 1/8 tsp.
1/4 fl.oz.	= 2 dram	= 1/2 tbsp.
1/2 fl.oz.	= 4 dram	= 1 tbsp.
3/4 fl.oz.	= 6 dram	= 1 tbsp + 1/2 tbsp.
1 fl.oz	= 8 dram	= 2 tbsp.

ॐ

Required Reading for This Chapter

Cunningham, Scott. *Cunningham's Encyclopedia of Magical Herbs*. Llewellyn, 1985.

———. *Magical Herbalism: The Secret Craft of the Wise*. Llewellyn, 1983.

ॐ

11

THE WHEEL OF THE YEAR

COUPLETS SIXTEEN AND SEVENTEEN of the Wiccan Rede teaches: "*When the wheel begins to turn, let the Beltane fires burn. When the wheel has turned to Yule, light the log an' the Horned One rules.*" This lesson permeates our being with imperative fundamental wisdom. First, it explains the importance of the seasonal changes of the year, and second, it shows how intricately connected we are to those seasonal changes as well as to our Gods.

The opening phrase, "*When the wheel begins to turn,*" refers to the Wheel of the Year, which is more or less a description of the pagan seasonal calendar. Pagans and Wiccans alike use the religious icon of the wheel to represent the cycle of seasons because, not only do the seasons revolve throughout the year like that of a wheel, but because within the wheel, one of the most holy and sacred shapes is manifest: *the circle.* The circle, and thusly the wheel, have always symbolized perfect balance without beginning or end. And so too do we see the balance of the seasons, being made up of the twelve months of the year, six being light and six being dark.

The second part of the sixteenth couplet is a bit of a misnomer. The line "*let the Beltane fires burn*," should actually have named Imbolc rather than Beltane, since Imbolc is often referred to as *Feast of Torches*.

Beltane is the Wiccan Sabbat celebrated by witches and pagans on April 30th (the eve of the actual holiday) or May 1st. This festival celebrates the coming of the warm months of summer as well as the marriage and union of the Goddess and God. Huge maypoles are normally erected, a phallic symbol of the God's increasing strength and his role as a fertility deity; the entire coven then commences to dance deosil around the maypole as part of the Beltane celebration. In the Germanic countries, Beltane is known as *Walpurgis*.

The seventeenth couplet, "*When the wheel has turned to Yule, light the log an' the Horned One rules*,"[1] speaks of the midwinter Sabbat, Yule, as well as our horned God of nature.

Yule is the winter solstice, and it falls between December 21st and December 23rd, depending on the

---

[1] *Cernunnos* and *Pan* are the deities that are usually honored in this celebration, since both are male Gods of the forest and woods, animals, and nature.

solar calendar of that specific year. The *Farmer's Almanac* usually has exact dates corresponding to the solar year and seasonal changes, so check that source for the precise days of the festival in your area. Yule symbolizes the birth of the Sun God by the Earth Goddess; it is celebrated by Wiccans and pagans alike.

Other Wiccan Seasonal Festivals

Samhain, or the *Feast of the Dead,* is the Sabbat celebrated by Wiccans and pagans on October 31st. This festival acknowledges the symbolic death of the Sun God[2] and awaits his rebirth from the Goddess, which occurs at Yule. It is customary to honor your deceased relatives and friends on this day. This is also considered the first day of the pagan year.

Imbolc, or the *Feast of Torches*, is the Sabbat that is celebrated by Wiccans and pagans on February 2nd. This festival celebrates the approaching springtime and acknowledges the recovery of our Mother Goddess from giving birth to our Sun God at Yule.

Ostara is the spring equinox. This Sabbat is celebrated between March 21st and March 23rd. Ostara

---

[2] The symbolic death of the Sun God is characterized by the dying off of vegetation from the approaching winter.

celebrates the return of our Sun God as He emerges from the darkness of winter. It is a time of joyful happiness and celebration, for the long cold months of winter are behind us and the warmth of the spring and summer lay ahead.

Litha falls on the summer solstice. This festival is often referred to as *Midsummer,* and is celebrated between June 21st and June 23rd. This festival celebrates the point of the year when our Sun God is at the height of His power. It is the longest day of the year and incidentally, one of the best days for the working of magick. If you planted a garden in April or May, by Litha, you should begin to see the fruits of your labors in the fresh young sprouts that have pushed up through the fertile soil.

Lughnasadh is celebrated on August 1st. This festival celebrates the first harvest and is a time of preparation for the coming winter months. Even though our God's power wanes, our Goddess' power increases during this time, and this too should be celebrated, for it is our Eternal Mother that will comfort and provide for us during the dark half of the year.

The autumn equinox is called Mabon. This Sabbat is celebrated between September 21st and September 23rd. Mabon acknowledges the second harvest of the year.

Esbats

Thus far, we have been discussing the Sabbats, which are best defined as being seasonal festivals, although they also acknowledge aspects of the solar year as well. Besides the Sabbats, Wiccans also observe the Esbats.

An Esbat is a Wiccan lunar celebration and is usually observed on the night of the full moon. Interesting to know, even though the months of the year number twelve, the total number of full moons occurring during the span of one year is thirteen. The *Farmer's Almanac* gives exact dates, not only of full moons, but also of the entire moon's cycles, so check this valuable source when scheduling your Esbat celebrations.

During an Esbat, one concentrates on the lunar aspects of our Eternal Mother, the Goddess.[3] Each celebration should represent the time of year that the celebration takes place, but one should focus more on deity than on season. Magick can be worked during the Esbat celebration, but it should come after the worship of our Goddess has commenced. Remember, Wicca is primarily a religion! As always, the main rites and ritu-

---

[3]If you have chosen a patron deity (ie: *Isis, Aphrodite, Hecate, Freya, etc.*), then proceed with her worship. If you have not chosen a patron deity, it is perfectly acceptable to worship our Mother in Her triune form of maiden, mother, and crone. As always, the choice is yours.

als of both Sabbat and Esbat should be preformed within a blessed circle.

For more information on circles, magick, and lunar cycles, please see the corresponding chapters in this manual.

Required Reading for This Chapter

Farrar, Stewart and Janet. *Eight Sabbats for Witches*. Robert Hale, 1981.

Slater, Herman. *A Book of Pagan Rituals*. Samuel Weiser, 1974.

12

OF DIVINATION
AND PROPHECY

THE NINETEENTH COUPLET of the Wiccan Rede teaches: "*Where the rippling waters go, cast a stone an' truth thou'll know*." This portion of the Rede's lesson is steeped in divination and prophecy. Not only do Wiccans perform magick to improve the quality of our lives, which is a birthright given to us as a gift by our Gods and Goddesses, but we also utilize divination to obtain information about our lives so that we can better work our magick for the betterment of the whole. By the use of certain divinatory techniques, the witch can gently spread the thin veil of the fabric of time and space and glimpse the future. By seeing into a possible future, we can better target our magickal energies, thus guaranteeing a higher degree of overall success in our magickal workings.

One thing to always keep in mind where divination and prophecy is concerned is this: *The future is not set in stone!* If it were, magick would simply not work. On the contrary, we are the ultimate controllers of our own destinies; for every second of every day we weave the ultimate web of our lives. As the Threefold Law teaches, whatever we do and however we act will have an impact on our lives. This goes for mundane activities as well as magickal workings. By taking the initiative, we can control our lives, and ultimately the world around us, and actually create our own future. Understanding this important fact is the first step in comprehending magick, divination, and the Wiccan Way; it is the beginning to seeing a much larger and greater illuminated world.

Another thing to remember: Divination and prophecy are not the same thing. Many people erroneously believe that the act of divination is prophecy. This is simply not true. Divination is the ability to glimpse the future by means of tools *outside* of one's self. By employing these outer tools, the witch must then decipher and interpret the signs. It takes much practice to become proficient at divination; it is not something that can be taught in three easy lessons.

On the other hand, prophecy is a *gift* from our Goddess[1] and her eternal consort, the God. This gift is

---

[1] In the Eddas, for example, it is the Goddess Freya who possesses the secrets of *Seidr*. She, in turn, granted this ability to the God Odin. This theme of the Goddess bestowing the gift of prophecy to the God recurs in many of the different myths and legends of various cultures of the world.

bestowed upon the individual by our Gods, and usually takes the form of dreams or visions. Unlike the many methods of divination, prophecy utilizes no outer tools, but rather, is an internal working sustained by the divine within one's self. To obtain the gift of prophecy, the witch can humbly petition the Goddess by means of a simple prayer. An example of this type of prayer can be seen below. Simply recite the prayer for three, six, or nine nights in a row, before retiring each evening.

A Prayer for Prophetic Dreams

"Divine Mother, You who were, are, and forever shall be; you who created everything from the nothingness of space; I ask that you grant me the gift of prophetic dreams so that I will be better equipped to deal with the ups and downs of my life as well as helping others in their times of need. Blessed be." [2]

When the gift of prophecy is bestowed, it will come in visions or dreams, but it is the ultimate responsibility of the witch to make use of these prophetic images. Some of these images will be slow in coming, and others will flood into one's psyche with an increasing magnitude that will seem to almost overload the mind.

---

[2] *"Prayer for Prophetic Dreams,"* page 128 of *The Wiccan Prayer Book*, Mark Ventimiglia, Citadel Press, 2000.

Do not try to control these images; simply see them and listen to what they tell you. While there is a degree of interpretation that must be employed, as in divination, prophecy is akin to a linking of the minds between you and your Gods; the images of a possible future will be much clearer than when utilizing the various methods of divination.

Divination

Divination, like numerology, herbology, magick, and many of the other occult subjects, would require a book many times larger than this current manual. To specialize in this incredible topic would involve countless lifetimes of intense study just to scratch the surface of its vast ocean of wisdom. A book of this scope cannot hope to contain a complete instructional section on divinatory skills and the various training methods employed by the myriad Wiccan traditions. It is my goal here to give the basic fundamentals of a few divinatory tools that are commonly used by Wiccans. Following are two of my favorite methods of divination. Simply experiment with the various methods and stick with the one that suits your needs. Everyone is different; therefore, there is no right or wrong method. The best advice: do what works best for you.

Pendulum

The use of the pendulum in divination is quite ancient. Typically, a pendulum consists of a crystal hanging from a cord. It can be in any shape but the material should come from the earth (crystal, precious metal, wood). The easiest technique for the beginner to master is the simple *yes-no* method. Obtain a 3 × 5-inch index card and draw a large plus sign at its center. Write the word *yes* on one perpendicular line, and the word *no* on the other, and then align the *yes line* according to the *northern axis*.

Now, ask a yes-no question and then hang the pendulum over the card, holding the chain as still as possible. Within a short time, the pendulum will begin to swing and you'll have your answer. It is as easy as that! After you have acquired a degree of skill using the above method, experiment with other techniques, such as holding the pendulum over maps when looking for lost objects, people, etc. You are limited only by your own imagination!

Skipping Stones

"*Where the rippling waters go, cast a stone an' truth thou'll know,*" refers to one of the oldest forms of divination known in European and American folklore, skipping stones across a lake. Simply go to a lake and ask a question, then skip a stone across the surface of the water, carefully counting the number of times the stone skips. If the number of skips is odd, then your answer is in the affirmative. If the stone skips an even number of times, then your answer is in the negative. You can customize this simple method of divination by modifying the procedure as well as the technique. One way to tailor this form of divination to suit your individual needs is to go to a *favorite* lake or pond.[3] You can also use a blessed stone, a holed stone,[4] or even a gemstone symbolic of your birth sign,[5] for an increased degree of success. Use your imagination, adapt a method that works best for you, and experiment often. Write down the results!

[3]It is important that the body of water being used has a serene surface as smooth as glass. Needless to say, fast moving bodies of water such as rivers, streams, and oceans, are counterproductive to this method of divination.

[4]A stone with a natural occurring hole through its center has long been considered sacred to our Goddess because it is symbolic of the female form.

[5]Zodiacal birthstones are not uncommon in most metaphysical shops and can be purchased relatively inexpensively. I would suggest that you refrain from using this method, save for only the most important reasons.

৶

Required Reading for This Chapter

Koch, Rudolph. *The Book of Signs*. Dover, 1955.
Lane, Julia. *The Numerology Workbook*. Sterling, 1985.

৶

13

OF MORALS AND ETHICS

THE TWENTIETH COUPLET of the Wiccan Rede teaches: "*When ye have an' hold a need, hearken not to others' greed.*" In this lesson, the Rede strays from its normal magickal instructions and proposes a wisdom teaching of moral and ethical proportions: teaching the basic differences between *need* and *greed*.

In today's world, especially in America and other major capitalistic countries, excess is the norm. The old saying "He who dies with the most toys wins" is very common in today's world and very clearly displays the level of greed present in the world today. The keeping-up-with-the-Joneses attitude has become almost subconscious and many of us do not even realize we are doing it.

The reason this selfishness has become subconscious is very simple to understand. Living in a market society, people have come to associate a higher standard of living with material goods. The big industries have capitalized on this idea by spending billions of dollars in advertising to bombard the consumer twenty-four hours a day with subliminal messages giving us reasons why we should buy their products. One company tells us we need their products to lose weight, another tells us that to be attractive we need to purchase their merchandise, and so on. Television commercials, newspaper ads, and huge billboards assault the eye as well as the intelligence. Most of us do our best to tune them out, but the messages are still received on a subconscious level and likewise continue to pollute our minds. Many companies have even added derogatory advertisements to their campaigns to give the illusion that more is better, when in fact the opposite is normally true.

Try this simple test: The next time you purchase something out of the ordinary, say, a new car, diamond ring, fancy dress, or suit, simply jot down the date of purchase, what it was you purchased, and the cost. Then look at your family and friends, work associates, and even strangers that you see regularly at health clubs, swim clubs, your doctor's office, etc. There is a big possibility that one of these other people made a big purchase just before you made yours. You are keeping up with the Joneses without even knowing it.

Once you realize how easy it is to fall into this trap of subconscious programming, you can then begin to deprogram yourself so you do not fall victim to it in the future. Too often success is measured by what a person *has* not by what a person *is*. The value of a person is not measured by how much money they have in their bank account, or the size of their house, or that expensive sports car in their driveway, but *who* and *what* they are. That is the most important thing. The true qualities of an individual's worth are their innate spiritual virtues: compassion, forgiveness, thoughtfulness, and selflessness. We all possess these virtues to one degree or another, yet in today's world they are suppressed due to the negative programming we are subject to throughout our life.

There are four basic necessities for life: food, water, shelter, and clothing. Anything that does not fall into these four basic categories are *wants*, not *needs*. Understanding the difference between a want and a need is the first step in gaining freedom from the materialistic bondage that most of us are experiencing.

How many of us shop when we are depressed? We think that by purchasing needless items and spending lots of hard-earned money we will alleviate our depression and become happy. But what really happens? We spend the money and find ourselves worse off because we are not only still depressed, but are now broke!

Please do not misunderstand the teachings of the Rede on this matter, nor take its wisdom out of context. The Rede does not say that food, water, shelter, and clothing are unnecessary, for on the contrary, these four items are indeed vital to living. The Rede is also not advocating the ascetic lifestyle, either. The teachings are quite clear, and when one fully realizes them enough to live by them, the quality of one's life is enhanced tenfold.

For instance, you need clothes. That is a basic life necessity. Clothing protects your physical body from the elements, thus guaranteeing you a measure of safety and well-being. But buying a two-thousand-dollar Armani suit is not really a necessity, is it? That is a luxury, a *want*. Certainly there are some people who can spend that kind of money without a bother, and that is fine. What we must understand is this: Just because one person has possessions that are more expensive than another's does not mean they are any happier than the person who has less. True happiness comes from within, not without. All the possessions in the world will not make you happy if you are not at peace with *who* you are!

Another problem with this subconscious greed programming—it was actually written into the U.S. Constitution over two hundred years ago! No idea in the history of humanity has caused as much suffering as the idea that one has the *right* to the pursuit of happiness. This concept has been wrongly interpreted as referring to the concept of Absolute Freedom, which I have already commented on earlier in this book. This idea, the practice of total freedom at the ultimate expense of others, is the physical manifestation of greed. When we look at the global economy, we can see that this concept is the root cause of all the world's problems. Large, wealthy countries are constantly exploiting small, poor countries, and consequently the entire world suffers, not just humanity, but the animals, forests, oceans, atmosphere, and the planet itself.

The secret to ultimate happiness is to practice Restrained Freedom. Break free from material bondage by living a selfless life and executing your free will, but not at the expense of others. This is the lesson that the Rede ultimately teaches. Strive to constantly live a mindful life by always asking yourself this simple question: *Do I cause suffering by doing this?* If the answer is yes, then re-evaluate your actions. By doing so, you not only alleviate the suffering of others, but you will also destroy your own suffering by living a greed-free, good karma life!

༈

Required Reading for This Chapter

Paxson, Diana. *The Wolf and the Raven*. Avon Books, 1993.
Tolkien, J. R. R. *The Hobbit*. Ballantine Books, 1966.

14

RELATIONSHIPS

THE TWENTY-FIRST COUPLET of the Wiccan Rede teaches: "*With a fool no season spend, lest ye be counted as her friend.*" Here we find the Rede giving us another commonsense teaching. Actually, the couplet is so completely self-explanatory that writing a complete chapter on the subject seems almost redundant. Still, the wisdom is founded on such timeless maxims as "You are judged by the company you keep" and "Birds of a feather flock together" and so we would do well to look deeply into the teachings of this very important part of the Rede.

Humanity, by and large, is made up of social creatures. We are herd animals; it is in our physical, mental, and spiritual makeup to associate with others of our kind. This, we have discovered through the advent of modern science, is healthy. For instance, science has discovered that the physical touch of a parent to its offspring has beneficial healing properties, as well as strengthing the overall endocrine system[1] of the baby. Physical contact, as well as audio and visual stimulation, also instills a degree of contentment in infants, thus strengthing their mental health. The same proves true in adults.

One look at various penal systems the world over and one will discover that solitary confinement is among the cruelest of punishments that can be administered to the human being. When a person is restricted from associating with others over a long period of time, certain physical, mental, and spiritual health problems arise. The Inochi Institute of St. Louis, Missouri, for example, has recently discovered that longstanding emotional problems such as repression of emotions and Social Anxiety Disorder can lead to actual physical health problems, such as blood deficiency and anemia. Participating in a positive social environment has been proven to be physically, spiritually, and mentally healthy.

The key word in the last sentence is *positive*. When we participate in a positive social environment, we are strengthening our overall health in a most beneficial way. Likewise, if our association with others is anything but positive, the effects are quite the opposite.

---

[1]The endocrine system is a glandular system in the physical body. Its function is to maintain proper health. Massage has been found to keep the endocrine system healthy.

There is something to be said for the selfless and compassionate person always looking to help the hard luck cases of society. These people are the true saints of the world. Yet, one must constantly remain on one's toes so as not to become overburdened with stress, which can destroy one's health as quickly as any disease. Knowing this, we should look at a definition of the term *fool* to obtain a complete understanding of where to begin our investigation of the twenty-first couplet of the Wiccan Rede.

The 1998 Oxford-American Desk Dictionary defines *fool* as "a person who acts unwisely or imprudently." The dictionary further defines a fool using such negative terms as "a trickster and a deceiver." Here we see two sides of the same coin. One definition is merely that of an unintelligent person blundering through life without direction; the other describes a calculated con artist, a vulture waiting to prey on unsuspecting individuals.

Taking these two definitions into account, the Rede's teachings become quite clear. As Wiccans, we constantly strive to live in harmony with nature. This is where the name *Wicca*[2] comes from, for to live in harmony with nature is the true essence of living wisely. In refraining

---

[2]The name *Wicca* comes from the old Anglo-Saxon term *Witta*, meaning "wise one." Wicca is often referred to as the *Religion of the Wise*.

from living a harmonious existence, one can be described as living unwisely, and hence, being foolish.

It is quite acceptable to associate with foolish people if your example is strong enough to help them advance in character and change for the better. But of course, if their foolish ways rub off on you, then you have allowed a grave injustice to yourself. Similarly, if you associate with criminals, and they cease their illegal activities because of your example, then you have done a great service to them. But on the other hand, if you fall onto their path, then you allow yourself to be judged a fool and are "guilty by association."

One thing to remember here is the phrase "to teach by example." This does not mean one should become preachy. Wicca is not a proselytizing religion by any means. Wiccans do not go door to door in the attempt to save souls, as do many of the big-business-type organized religions. We follow a simple path and our actions certainly speak louder than any word. When one teaches by example, another is not even conscious of the teaching. Simply to live in harmony with nature, co-existing in a peaceful manner with all of creation, is truly being wise.

So, as the Rede says, *"With a fool no season spend, lest ye be counted as her friend."* One important thing to always keep in mind when in the company of foolish people is this: *By living the Wiccan Rede and through teaching by example one can help transform one's foolish friends into wise friends.* That is the true essence of being a real friend!

ॐ

Required Reading for This Chapter

Paxson, Diana. *The Dragons of the Rhine.* Avon Books, 1995.
————. *The Lord of Horses.* Avon Books, 1996.

ॐ

15

UNCONDITIONAL LOVE

THE TWENTY-SECOND COUPLET of the Wiccan Rede teaches: "*Merry meet an' merry part, bright the cheeks an' warm the heart.*" This couplet is much more than a folkish salutation; it is a lesson in friendship and unconditional love.

Wicca is a gentle faith, and love is at the heart of our religion. Love, and a respect for *all* life, not just human life, are the main motivating principles behind Wicca, and likewise, this unconditional love controls our actions. However, this control is not a binding restraint, but a pure freedom of expression, choice, and free will. When we love unconditionally, and live our daily life through the actions of that love, our heart is light and our mind is clear; we then experience a freedom unlike anything explainable in words.

We practicing Wiccas must be ever conscious of our actions, in everything we do. This is especially true when dealing with non-Wiccans, and even more so if they know we are Wiccan and are not sympathetic to our religion. In today's world, religious prejudice is everywhere and we should be aware of this, but we should not let it affect us in a negative way. We should act toward everyone as if they are a true friend, regardless of how they feel toward us. Living this way, we not only strengthen our own good karma, but we teach by example as well.

Of course, it is easier to deal with our Wiccan friends. They do not look down their noses at us for being different, nor do they try to convert us to their way of thinking. Surrounding yourself with a circle of like-minded Wiccan friends is better than any support group, and if the circle of friends evolves into a working coven, then all the better!

Whether you see another on the road, or invite them into your home for a visit, always greet them with the warm and cheerful phrase, *"Merry Meet!"* This greeting breaks the ice with new acquaintances and rekindles the flame of love in old friends. And likewise, upon bidding a friend farewell, the loving term *"Merry Part"* will always bring a smile. You might even get a hug and a kiss out of it too!

"Merry Part" is more than a simple good-bye, for in those two tiny words a multitude of emotion is shared as one is confirming the fact that the visit was not only pleasant and enjoyable, but magickally fulfilling as well.

As wonderful as our friends are, it is a sad reality that they cannot be with us every second of the day. Therefore, the time we spend together we cherish deeply and the time apart we must learn to endure. Below is a simple prayer to our eternal mother and father, the Goddess and God of all creation. Know that They are not only your mother and father, but your friends' eternal parents as well. Asking Them to watch over and protect your family and friends will allow you peace of mind when separated from your loved ones, as well as strengthen the bonds to all facets of your spiritual and magickal family.

"*Dear eternal parents, I know that you are the mother and father of all creation. I know that we are all one family. I thank you for my friends, who are my brothers and sisters in your love. Please protect and watch over them when we are apart. So mote it be.*"[1]

꒳

Required Reading for This Chapter

Tolkien, J. R. R. *The Fellowship of the Ring*. Ballantine Books, 1965.

———. *The Return of the King*. Ballantine Books, 1983.

———. *The Two Towers*. Ballantine Books, 1982.

[1] Ventimiglia, Mark. *The Wiccan Prayer Book*. Citadel Press, 2000.

16

THE THREEFOLD LAW

THE TWENTY-THIRD COUPLET of the Wiccan Rede teaches: "*Mind the Threefold Law ye should, three times bad an' three times good.*" This important lesson is speaking mainly of the Wiccan Law of Retribution. One must understand that the Rede is not a set of laws that must not be transgressed in fear of eternal damnation, but rather a gentle reminder of the nature of things in our world and how they work.

When we are speaking on the topic of retribution, it is to be understood that this *Rule of Three* is retribution in action. But contrary to many other religious traditions, where rules are simply a guarantee for punishment, the Rule of Three can work as a positive force as well as a negative force. This means that if you do evil, then evil will return to you threefold. Likewise, if you perform good works, then three times the goodness will return to you.

Of course, this concept seems simple enough, but how many of us really follow these teachings? Many books and teachers teach this Law insignificantly, speaking only of the astral and etheric planes rather than the physical plane. Indeed, all planes of existence are important and any action, regardless of where that action is executed, has karmic reactions, rewards, and consequences.

Most witches contemplate long and hard before casting spells and working magick, careful not to violate the Threefold Law, but what about the mundane, physical world? Do we really spend enough time thinking about our actions when we are not thinking about Wicca or magick? Remember the most important line of the Rede: "*An it harm none.*" These four simple words sum up the entire Rede in a nutshell, and reciting them daily can generate many rewards, as well as eliminate the side effects of negative karmic reactions due to mindlessness. Whether we realize it or not, ignorance of our actions is not a safeguard from them. No matter what we do, we are held responsible. Take, for instance, this scenario: You are driving your car down a quiet road. Perhaps the radio is up a bit, or maybe you are going a little too fast. In a blank of an eye, a tiny squirrel darts out in front of you and before you can swerve or stop, you hear the thud of a little body bouncing under your car. Of course you feel sick, but what could you have done, right? It was an accident. You just keep on driving, even after seeing the tiny body lying lifeless in the road in your rearview mirror.

Now, what if that squirrel wasn't a squirrel, but a small child? You couldn't just keep driving, for there would be police reports and questions, many questions. The main question that everyone would ask would be "Was the accident your fault?" Who's to blame? Of course, you could petition the courts, plead your case, and hope for the best. Maybe things would work out in your favor, maybe not. The fact of the matter would remain that, due to something *you* did, a life has been taken. It would not matter whether or not you were at fault, nor would it matter between animal or human. The outcome would be the same—a life has been taken and retribution will be extracted.

The Law of Retribution isn't so cut and dried. Ignorance does not excuse one from karmic reactions, neither does innocence or accident. What happens, happens. It is as simple as that. Many people, witches included, might argue with me on this matter, but hear me out. The Law of Retribution is not a law like the Judeo-Christian Ten Commandments. It is not a law that was created by man, but is, rather, a natural law akin to the Law of Gravity or the Law of Inertia.

All natural laws, whether one is ignorant of them or not, affect each individual. Take the Law of Gravity.

Gravity affects everyone regardless of whether they understand the law or not. A small child does not understand the intricacies of physics, but if she trips and stumbles, the Law of Gravity affects her and she falls. All laws of nature work in this manner. There is no exception. This is why we must be careful to weigh all of our actions, not just our magickal ones.

So, regarding the Threefold Law, we should always ask ourselves the simple question: *Am I harming anyone or anything by doing this?* If you can honestly answer in the negative, then you are probably safe to continue, but be sure you weigh all the possibilities.

On the lighter side of things, we can see that by working good deeds the rewards will be significantly greater. Everything, according to the Threefold Law, comes back on us three times over. Well, then it should go without saying that we should constantly strive to do good. Perhaps carrying out the trash for Mom and Dad could be your good deed. To go one better than that, not only carry out the trash, but separate and recycle the garbage as well. This way you are not only doing a good deed for your parents, but you are helping keep Mother Nature clean too! Constantly use your imagination to come up with better ways to do good deeds, and the rewards will come to you like you never imagined.

One thing to keep in mind when performing your good deeds: *Do them selflessly*. Don't execute good deeds with the sole intention of getting something out of it. Of course, according to the Threefold Law, your rewards will come regardless of the motive, but still, to advance spiritually one should always perform good deeds with a selfless attitude and an open heart.

Required Reading for This Chapter

LeGuin, Ursula K. *A Wizard of Earthsea*. Bantam, 1968.

17

THE PENTAGRAM

THE TWENTY-FOURTH COUPLET of the Wiccan Rede teaches: *"When misfortune is enow, wear the witches' star on thy brow."* When contemplating the teachings of this couplet it would be a good idea for the neophyte Wiccan, as well as the seasoned witch, to go back and re-read Chapters Three and Six, for the power of the *witches' star* is bound up in our supremely magickal and religious symbol, the pentagram.

Many uninformed people will claim this is the sign of evil. Some people will go even further and say it is the mark of the devil. All of this is complete and utter nonsense. First, the pentagram is anything but evil. The five-pointed star is merely a symbol of the *Five Powers*, namely earth, air, fire, water, and spirit. Everything in our material universe is comprised of these five elements and revering this star is a Wiccan method of confirming this deeply spiritual belief. Secondly, the so-called devil is a Judeo-Christian invention and has no place in the Wiccan religion. So, claiming that *our* symbol represents *their* devil is complete ignorance. It also leads to the spiritually degrading practice of religious prejudice.

Furthermore, some religiously closed-minded individuals have even concluded that inverting the penta-

gram adds to its evil and baneful properties. However, nothing could be further from the truth. While it is a fact that some unscrupulous religions, such as Satanism, constantly try to gain notoriety by degrading other religious practices, such as wearing inverted crosses and pentagrams, one must keep in mind that Wicca is *not* Satanism. Our gentle faith is based on a deep love and respect for Mother Earth and Father Spirit. We do not honor or worship any evil entity. This being said, let us now move on to the true essence and wisdom of this couplet's lesson.

Looking closely at the couplet, we can see that the pentagram is indeed a strong tool for protection from misfortune. The main reason this is true is because it comprises everything in existence: *earth, air, fire, water, and spirit*. Our physical bodies are made up of earth and water elements, while the elements of air and fire[1] keep us alive. Of course, our etheric and astral bodies are comprised of spirit. If we look deeply at the intricate workings of these five sacred elements, we will be able to understand that we are truly a part of a larger organism. We are connected with everything in the universe and everything in the universe is connected with us. Once this is comprehended on a deep and spiritual level, true *spiritual* enlightenment takes place and you will see the world as it truly is for the first time, unhindered by the biasness of prejudice and ignorance.

---

[1] We need air to breathe in order to survive, and our warm-blooded, 98.6-degree body temperature is proof enough that the element of fire is at work sustaining our health.

Even though our material work is a wonderful and magickal place, there are many dangers lurking that can cause physical, mental, and spiritual harm. Therefore, it is a smart practice to begin using the pentagram as a means to safeguard one's self, as well as one's family and friends. Below are a few suggestions and minor enchantments that you can cast to help protect you and your loved ones from misfortune by using the *witches' star*.

Protecting the Home

On a 3×3-inch circular piece of ash or oak wood, simply engrave the five-pointed star with your athame during the full moon. When finished, consecrate the pentagram with salt, blessed water, and incense, in the name of your patron deity, and then nail it to the front door of your house. You can increase the star's effectiveness by incorporating color magick into the spell. For example, if you seek to guard against illness, simply paint the pentagram blue; for love, red; for wealth, green.

Protecting the Kitchen

Obtain a small glass jar, and paint a pentagram on its outer surface. Then fill the jar with blessed salt and store in the cupboard. Your kitchen will be protected as long as the jar remains in place.

Protecting Food

To guard against food poisoning of any kind, simply get into the habit of magickally inscribing a pentagram in the dishes, pots, and pans that you use in your cooking. You don't have to actually carve into the utensils! Actually, just use the index finger of your power (dominant) hand to trace the star. It is as simple as that. You can also do this with a wooden spoon or ladle when you are making soup, stew, chili, etc.

Protecting Your Pets

To protect your beloved pets, simply get a blank pet tag from your veterinarian or the local pet store, inscribe a pentagram on it, then attach it to your pet's collar. They will be safe and secure!

These are just a few examples of how you can use the witches' star to guard and protect yourself and those you love with the magickally powerful pentagram. Use your imagination and your magick will know no bounds!

༃

Required Reading for This Chapter

Blamires, Steve. *Glamoury: Magic of the Celtic Green World.* Llewellyn, 1991.

Conway, D. J. *Falcon Feather and Valkyrie Sword.* Llewellyn, 1992.

18

OF FIDELITY AND TRUST

THE TWENTY-FIFTH COUPLET of the Wiccan Rede
teaches: "*True in love forever be, lest thy lover's false to thee.*"
This important lesson is reminiscent of the teachings of
Lesson One in the first couplet, and one would do well
to go back and review that lesson after studying this
short chapter.

Recapping the teachings in Lesson One, we can
easily understand that if we truly abide in perfect love
and perfect trust, we will then know the ultimate
meaning of the phrase, "*True in love forever be, lest thy
lover's false to thee.*"

As in the teaching of the first couplet, this couplet's
lesson goes further than love and recaps the ultimate
foundation of love, which is trust. As I have said before,
love and trust coexist eternally within the boundaries of
loyalty. To love unconditionally is to remain forever
faithful in that love, and where there is unconditional
love, there is also unconditional trust. We must never
do anything that will violate that trust.

"True in love forever be, lest thy lover's false to thee," sums up this idea of loyalty perfectly, but also adds an ultimatum. While Chapter One dealt primarily with love in general, the twenty-fifth couplet clearly defines the bonds of marital love. The Rede clearly states that one should remain forever loyal to one's partner; however, if the other is unfaithful to you, then by all means, the relationship can be severed and the two may go their separate ways. In today's world of domestic violence and nasty divorces, much wisdom can be had from this simple and timeless teaching, and much suffering can be alleviated. Even if the marriage must end in a hand-parting,[1] one should execute a good degree of love in that parting. The old maxim that teaches we should be strong enough in our love to be able to set our partner free holds true.[2] While I can personally attest to the difficulty of honoring this statement, and the incredible amount of strength it takes, it is the best advice available. No one ever said loving unconditionally would be easy!

When one takes up the practice of Wicca, and the responsibility of entering into a Wiccan handfasted[3]

---

[1] Wiccan rite of divorce.

[2] If you love something, set it free. If it comes back to you, it is yours. If it doesn't, it never was.

[3] Wiccan rite of marriage.

relationship, one must always be conscious of the family one is creating. Whether it is just the two being handfasted, or there are children involved, it should be understood that we must always act in love toward our partner, for that love is a reflection of our love toward the Goddess and the God, as well as all of creation. There is an eternal bond of love and trust that originates from such a spiritual relationship and fulfilling that love and trust will not only bring both partners closer together but will also strengthen the bond of love between them, their family, and their Goddess and the God.

Required Reading for This Chapter

Gardner, Gerald B. *Witchcraft Today*. Rider, 1954.

19

HARM NONE

THE TWENTY-SIXTH AND FINAL COUPLET of the
Wiccan Rede teaches: *"Eight words the Wiccan Rede fulfill: An ye harm none, do as thou will."* This lesson is the
foundation on which the Rede, and the entire religion
of Wicca, is built. *"An ye harm none, do as thou will"* is a
simple but very powerful philosophy. To live this lesson
on a daily basis is to completely exist in a state of *conscious compassion*, ever mindful of your own actions and
how those actions affect others.

Common to the religious beliefs of many North
American Indian[1] tribes is the *Seven Generations Rule*. This
rule is very similar to the underlying theme of this chapter's lesson. The Seven Generations Rule states that one
should be forever conscious of their actions, but it goes
much further than that. Each person must evaluate their
actions, and the repercussions of those actions, into the

[1] All of the aboriginal Native American Indian tribes practiced the
nature-revering religion of shamanism. Wicca is a form of shamanism and
there are many similarities between Wicca and other shamanistic religions.

future for seven generations. What this means is simple: Think about whatever it is that you are getting ready to do. *Will that action harm anyone, or anything?* Now take it one step further and examine whether the action will do any harm to future generations. Now push this examination seven generations into the future. If you can go seven generations into the future without causing harm, then you are safe to proceed with that action.

While this lesson of the Rede does not seem as strict as the Native American *Seven Generation Rule*, one can still learn from the selflessness and conscious compassion of the great Native Americans.

Many modern-day, die-hard Wiccans might argue the point against the Native Americans, claiming that they hunted and killed many animals for food and clothing and therefore were not compassionate. However, one must remember that centuries ago humanity did not possess the technology to create synthetic clothing[2] or meat substitutes,[3] therefore the Native Americans had

---

[2] Today's synthetic clothing is far superior to authentic leather and fur and the practicing Wiccan would do well to support this cruelty-free industry.

[3] Veggie-patch.com and Lightlife.com are two fabulous companies that specialize in meat substitutes. I have personally served their fare to meat eaters for years, all of whom have commented on how they could not tell the difference between the veggie meat and the real thing. The only two differences being that the food is lower in cholesterol and fats, thereby being healthier, and that no animals had to suffer and die.

no choice but to hunt and kill for their survival. Of course, inevitably, there was some negative karma that was generated, but they understood that, they understood the way of nature and what would be expected of them in regards to their actions. In comparison to modern humanity's meat, leather, silk, and fur industries, where billions upon billions of innocent animals are killed for the greed of our bellies, tongues, and fashion, there can be no doubt that the Native Americans lived a consciously compassionate life.

So, how does all of this translate to our present world and the life you want to live? Well, that depends entirely on you. The nice thing about Wicca is that the religion gives one the freedom to live life to the fullest, as long as one practices self-restraint. Again, there are some who may protest this selfless attitude, claiming that to restrain one's self is not true freedom. I beg to differ. When one practices restrained freedom,[4] as opposed to absolute freedom,[5] one's mind and conscience is completely devoid of guilt or any other undesirable and negative emotion. True spiritual freedom is experienced as a result of such a lifestyle.

---

[4] *Restrained freedom* is the practice of living a free life and executing one's free will but not at the expense of others.

[5] *Absolute freedom* is the practice of total freedom at the ultimate expense of others.

Below are a few examples of how you can engage in a life of conscious compassion and truly live the Wiccan Rede on a daily basis. You will be amazed at the difference it will make in your life, physically, mentally, and spiritually.

Prayer as a Means to Heal Mother Earth

When trying to live a cruelty-free life, many people consistently try to refrain from doing things such as eating meat, wearing leather or fur, and buying products that were tested on animals. But very few people think of things they *can* do to help ease the suffering. Prayer is the easiest, quickest, and usually the most effective thing a person can do to alleviate the problems of the world. One can recite a prayer to cleanse the air and water, or perhaps say a prayer to heal the earth. In today's world, due to humanity's greed, there is much more suffering than just that experienced by the animals. Our forests are being eliminated at an alarming rate, the oceans are thick with sludge and pollution, and the air we breathe is filled with smog and poisons. A simple prayer to our Lord and Lady on a daily basis will work wonders toward curbing these problems.

But don't just stop there; say a prayer for humanity as well. A simple prayer to end world hunger or to increase the compassion of our lawmakers and national leaders will go a long way toward repairing our troubled world.

These prayers can be recited from a prayer book, or they can be self-composed and in your own words. Remember, it is the intent that is important, not the words. Speak to the God and Goddess sincerely and from your heart and your prayer will be heard and answered.

Environment Protection

Most of us get completely overwhelmed when we think about all the many problems of the world. Even though the world's problems seem at times astronomical, there are still many things we can do to lend a helping hand. One of the easiest and health-effective things one can do is buy a *push mower!*

The American Lawn Mower Company manufactures a wonderful engineless lawn mower for under one hundred dollars.[6] No engine means no gas, and hence, no pollution! There are other benefits as well. For one, no gas means cheaper operating costs. Actually, other than

---

[6] Most hardware stores carry American Lawn Mower brand lawn mowers.

an occasional squirt of oil, you can run the machine for free! The lawn mower is also extremely quiet. At a distance of about fifteen feet one can barely even hear the clipping of the blades. Your neighbors will love you, especially if you are in the habit of cutting the grass early on Saturday morning! And lastly, with no motor, you will exert a bit more muscle to complete the job and this results in better overall health. Why go to the spa when you can get a good workout, a tan, and your lawn mowed all at once?

Plant Trees

Another thing the practicing Wiccan can do to better the world and help heal rather than hurt is join your local chapter of the National Audubon Society. Most cities and towns in the U.S. have active chapters of this fine organization where the volunteer member can go out with other members on tree-planting missions. You will be doing a wonderful service, for trees are nature's way of cleaning the air.

These are but a fraction of the things you can do to live a life of conscious compassion in accord with the teachings of the Wiccan Rede. There are many, many more things you can do, and you are only limited by the scope of your own imagination. To *be* a Wiccan means to become *one with nature*, and to become one with nature means to live in harmony with all of creation and to never cause harm to anyone or anything, including yourself. When one practices such a lifestyle, one experiences the full bounty of our Lord and Lady, and a fullness of life that defies explanation.

Required Reading for This Chapter

Ventimiglia, Mark. *The Wiccan Prayer Book*. Citadel Press, 2000.
The Healthy Planet Magazine.

Conclusion

THE TWENTY-SIX COUPLETS of the Wiccan Rede are similar to the eighty-one poems of the *Tao Te Ching*. They are comprised of a timeless wisdom and yet complete in and of themselves. One can spend a lifetime of study and still not scratch the surface of their meaning, for only with an open mind and a sincere heart can their true essence be grasped.

The long version of the Rede is quite a lot to memorize, and even the most die-hard Wiccans still don't have it confined to memory. But don't fret, the entire wisdom of our gentle faith is also summed up in the short version of the Rede and can be memorized easily. Personally, I use this short version as a daily affirmation of my faith and recite it many times a day.

WICCAN REDE: SHORT VERSION[1]

Bide the Wiccan Law ye must,
In perfect love, in perfect trust.
Eight words the Wiccan Rede fulfill:
An' ye harm none, do as ye will.

[1] Ventimiglia, Mark. *The Wiccan Prayer Book.* Citadel Press, 2000.

An' ever mind the Rule of Three:
What ye sends out comes back to thee.
Follow this with mind and heart,
An' merry ye meet, an' merry ye part.

One last thing I would like to mention before closing this manual is this: *Being Wiccan means living the Rede daily.* And that translates into practicing the religion, not just reading about it. Too often, at lectures and workshops, I have heard people say, "Oh yes, I am Wiccan." When I ask them what makes them Wiccan, they nonchalantly reply, "Well, I read a book on Wicca and liked it so much I now consider myself a Wiccan."

While reading books and studying about the religion is a good starting point, it is not enough. One must practice the tenets of the faith on a daily basis to truly *be* Wiccan. And isn't that what religion is all about anyway—changing your lifestyle, physically as well as spiritually, for the better?

I hope this manual has enriched your life, answered your questions about Wicca, and brought you closer to your God and Goddess. May they always reside in your heart and mind.

Blessed be.

GLOSSARY

Absolute freedom: The practice of total freedom at the ultimate expense of others.

Amenhotep III: Pharaoh of the XVIII Dynasty who created the first monotheistic religious system. Amenhotep IV followed his predecessor's example and under his reign, Egypt remained monotheistic. Egypt did not seem to do very well under the guise of monotheism and did not adhere to it for very long, for when Tutankhamen ascended the throne as Pharaoh, he abolished monotheism and reinstated polytheism. See also *Aton cult*.

Animism: Animism and shamanism are nature-respecting religious philosophies where a spirit, or a god, is attributed to each of the forces of nature. Simply put, one god controls the wind, another god controls the rain, a different god controls the growth of vegetation, and so on. See also *Shamanism*.

Athame: The athame is the ritual knife used by the witch during magickal spellworkings.

Aton cult: The first monotheistic religion. See also *Amenhotep III*.

Beltane: Sabbat celebrated by Wiccans and pagans on April 30th or May 1st. This festival celebrates the coming of summer and the union of the Goddess and God. In the Germanic countries, it is known as *Walpurgis*.

Book of Shadows: Personal spellbook of modern-day witches containing rituals and magickal instructions. See also *Grimoire*.

Bubonic plague: The Black Death. This disease killed millions during Europe's dark ages.

Cartomancy: Fortune-telling by means of cards.

Cernunnos: Horned God of nature.

Christianity: Middle-Eastern monotheistic religious cult that came into existence approximately two thousand years ago, after breaking away from Judaism.

Circle: Religious icon symbolizing perfect balance without beginning or end.

Deosil: Sun-wise or clockwise.

Duality, Principle of: Philosophic principle of polarities as seen in the male-female energy of nature.

Eddas and Sagas: Ancient Teutonic mythological tales.

Elder Futhark: A system of runology used by those of the Norse tradition.

Esbat: An Esbat is a Wiccan lunar celebration and is usually observed on the full moon.

Folk magic: Simple and informal magickal techniques practiced by pagan country people, as opposed to the highly formal and ritualized ceremonial magick usually practiced by groups or covens.

Formularies: Books containing magickal formulas and recipes such as ritual oils, incense, brews, etc. See also *Grimoire*.

Futhorc: A system of rune magick.

Garden of Eden: Mythical land supposedly located in the Middle East between the Tigris and Euphrates Rivers, put forth in the Judeo-Christian Bible as the place where God created the first human being.

Ginnungagap: The primal seed for all matter. According to the Eddas, everything emerged from Ginnungagap, the Great Void.

God-force: The primal, life-spawning energy of the cosmos as personified by a male-female polarity.

Grimoire: Ancient magickal spellbook or *Book of Shadows*. See also *Formularies*.

Herbology: The science of herbs.

Imbolc: Sabbat celebrated by Wiccans and pagans on February 2nd. This festival celebrates the approaching springtime and acknowledges the recovery of the mother Goddess from giving birth to the Sun God at Yule.

Islam: Middle-Eastern monotheistic religious cult.

Jehovan cult: Middle-Eastern monotheistic religious cult that was founded by Moses and structured after the Egyptian Aton cult. See also *Amenhotep III* and *Aton cult*.

Judaism: Middle-Eastern monotheistic religious cult.

Litha: Midsummer Sabbat (summer solstice) celebrated by Wiccans and pagans on June 21st. This festival celebrates the point of the year when the Sun God is at the height of his power. It is the longest day of the year and one of the best days for the working of magick.

Lucy: The Lucy fossils were discovered by D. C. Johanson on the surface of Pliocene deposits in Ethiopia. They are the oldest human fossils ever found and are around four million years old.

Lughnasadh: Sabbat celebrated by Wiccans and pagans on August 1st. This festival celebrates the first harvest. This is a time of preparation for the coming winter months when the God's power wanes and the Goddess' power increases.

Mabon: Sabbat celebrated by Wiccans and pagans on September 21st. This festival celebrates the autumn equinox and the second harvest.

Magick: Supernatural ability latent in the human psyche that allows the practitioner to cause change to occur in the material world as according to one's Will.

Malleus Maleficarum: Medieval Christian tome that outlined the torture requirements to be exacted on suspected witches. See also *Witch Hammer*.

Mithraism: Middle-Eastern monotheistic religious cult.

Monotheism: Religious system that centers around a single, male God.

Moses: Ancient Egyptian warrior who left Egypt to found his own religious order, the monotheistic Jehovah cult. See also *Amenhotep III*, *Aton cult*, *Jehovah cult*, and *Monotheism*.

New Age: A user-friendly, politically correct term for the alternative spiritual practices of modern-day occultists.

New Testament: Collection of books in the Christian Bible that predominantly centers around the birth, life, and death of Christ.

Numerology: The occult science of numbers.

Occult: Greek word meaning "that which is hidden." Secret wisdom; supernatural knowledge; magick.

Old Testament: Oldest collection of books in the Judeo-Christian Bible.

Ostara: Sabbat celebrated by Wiccans and pagans on March 21st. This festival celebrates the spring equinox and the return of the Sun God as He emerges from the darkness of winter.

Pagan: An individual who practices paganism.

Paganism: A folk-styled, earth-based, nature-respecting, shamanistic religion; the Old Religion.

Pan: Horned God of the woods.

Papyrus of Nu: An XVIII Dynasty funerary scroll and part of the Egyptian *Book of the Dead*.

Pentagram: The pentagram is the five-pointed star commonly used in the magickal workings of many traditions. Symbolically, it refers to the five magickal elements of earth, air, fire, water, and spirit.

Personal Power Number: The number of an individual as calculated by the sum of their Primary Life Number and their Secondary Life Number.

Polytheism: Religious system of beliefs that center around a pantheon of many Gods and deities.

Power hand: Your power hand is the hand you use the most. If you write with your left hand, then your left hand is your power hand. Ambidextrous people can use either hand as their power hand.

Primary Life Number: The number of an individual as calculated using one's birth date.

Ragnarok: The story of the end of the world as mentioned in the *Eddas*.

Restrained freedom: The practice of living a free life and executing one's Free Will but not at the expense of others.

Sabbat: A Sabbat is a Wiccan festival and pertains to seasonal times of the year such as Beltane, Imbolc, Samhain, and Yule.

Samhain: Sabbat celebrated by Wiccans and pagans on October 31st. This festival celebrates the feast of the dead as the Sun God symbolically dies and awaits rebirth from the Goddess at Yule.

Satan: Christian invention of an all-evil deity or God.

Seax Wiccan runes: Runic *Futhorc* utilized by the Seax-Wicca, a Saxon tradition of Witchcraft that was re-created by Raymond Buckland in 1973.

Secondary Life Number: The number of an individual as calculated by one's name.

Seidr: The magickal act of entering a trance and divining the future. Seidr can also be employed as a means to shapeshift, work magick, etc.

Shaman: One who practices shamanism.

Shamanism: Shamanism is a nature-respecting religion where a spirit, or a god, is attributed to each of the natural forces of nature. See also *Animism*.

Spell: A magickal working, i.e., *To cast a spell*.

Ten Commandments: Mosaic Law of the Jehovah cult.

Theban alphabet: An arcane system of writing created in the seventeenth century, and erroneously referred to as the Witch's runes. Also called *Wiccan Runes*.

Thought-form: A thought-form is a psychic phenomenon that is created by the mental and emotional beliefs of an individual or society. Where this belief is concentrated, through the adherence of religious and magickal rites by practitioners, the thought-form grows in strength and intelligence until it becomes an independent and conscious entity.

Threefold Law: Wiccan Law of Retribution.

Wheel: Religious icon symbolizing perfect balance without beginning or end.

Wicca: Modern polytheistic magickal religious system relating to the traditions of witchcraft.

Wiccan: One who practices Wicca.

Wiccan Rede: Basic law of the Wiccan religion.

Wiccan Runes: See *Theban alphabet*.

Widdershins: Counterclockwise.

Wights: Helpful spirits.

Witchcraft: The Old Religion; original shamanistic religious and magickal system of the human race. See also *Animism* and *Shamanism*.

Witch Hammer: In 1486, two German Christian monks, Heinrich Kramer and Jakob Sprenger, published their infamous Medieval Christian tome *Malleus Maleficarum*, the *Witch Hammer*, which graphically outlined many heinous torture techniques to be used on individuals suspected of witchcraft. See also *Malleus Maleficarum*.

Yggdrasill: Yggdrasill is the great Ash, or the World Tree, that supports the Nine Worlds of the Teutonic cosmos.

Yule: Midwinter Sabbat (winter solstice) celebrated by Wiccans and pagans on December 21st. This festival celebrates the birth of the Sun God from the Earth Goddess.

Zoroaster: Zoroaster was a Persian religious leader living in the seventh century B.C.E. who invented the doctrine of a one *all good* god and one *all evil* god.

✝ɴᴅᴇx

ABOUT THE AUTHOR

MARK VENTIMIGLIA was born in Alton, Illinois, in July of 1965. He has devoted more than half his life to seeking spiritual wisdom and has studied most of the world's major religious traditions as well as many pagan and shamanistic traditions. Mark was ordained by the Universal Life Church in 1995 and earned his Ph.D. in religious philosophy in 1996. Since 1997, he has given lectures and workshops on the Wiccan religion and alternative spirituality. Mark continues to work hard to break down the walls of religious prejudice and ignorance that undermine harmony and love in today's society.

Mark Ventimiglia can be e-mailed at mark71565@ yahoo.com for book signings, public events, lectures, and workshop information and scheduling.